CZECH ROUTES

Selected Czechoslovak artists in Britain from the Ben Uri and private collections

Editor
Nicola Baird

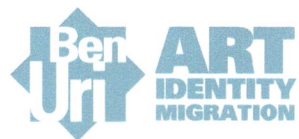

Ben Uri Research Unit for the Study of the Jewish and Immigrant Contribution to the Visual Arts in Britain since 1900

Acknowledgements

This exhibition would not have been possible without the engagement of a number of private collectors and contributors and I would like to thank the following individuals for their support and goodwill: Tereza Bušková, Mila Fürstová, Benjamin Midgley, Tereza Stehliková, Caroline Uhlman and those wishing to remain anonymous as well as The Franta Bělský Estate and The Irena Sedlecká Studio. Thanks are also due to Ben Uri colleagues Rachel Dickson, David Glasser, Sarah MacDougall and Alix Smith.

I would particularly like to thank the authors for their original contributions: Peter Cannon-Brookes and Caroline Cannon-Brookes.

Thanks are also due to the catalogue designer Alan Slingsby and photographer Justin Piperger.

Nicola Baird

July 2019

ISBN 978-0-900157-68-4

Contents

Chairman's Foreword

Czech Routes is the fourth in Ben Uri's current series of exhibitions designed to highlight the contribution of immigrant artists to Britain since 1900, succeeding previous exhibitions on German, Austrian and Polish artists in 2016, 2017 and 2018. This occasion also marks the formal opening of the reconfigured museum and its extensive art reference library and archive, both key components of BURU, the Ben Uri Research Unit for the study of the Jewish and immigrant contribution to the visual arts in Britain since 1900, and we are delighted that *Czech Routes* is, therefore, also BURU's inaugural exhibition.

Ben Uri Gallery and Museum was founded in 1915 as a Jewish arts society in London's East End by Russian-Jewish immigrant artist Lazar Berson. After 80 years celebrating the work of Jewish artists and, in its last decades, almost entirely positioned for and within the London Jewish community, Ben Uri lost its Soho gallery in 1995. Drawing on both its rich history and a new vision for its future, a new team then re-launched Ben Uri in a small gallery in St John's Wood in 2002. It continues to proudly represent the Jewish community, but now from within the mainstream British arts sector, the biggest difference being that artists born into the Jewish faith are now addressed within the artistic rather than religious context and displayed alongside their artist peers (irrespective of ethnicity). Since then, our focus has continued to widen to address and research the wider artistic contribution of immigrants to Britain since 1900, alongside that of Jewish artists. We

have also qualitatively grown the collection to reflect this wider contribution.

Thinking differently about how a small, niche, consistently financially challenged art museum survives and delivers distinctive public benefit in the most competitive cultural city in the world, Ben Uri has continued to adjust and finesse its positioning within the arts and charity sector. In 2015 our centenary exhibition, held at Kings Cultural Centre at Somerset House, London, was attended by over 30,000 visitors. When in 2017, however, a long-planned merger with a distinguished arts centre and university fell through, the Trustees embarked on a major review to craft a purposeful and productive future for the charity.

The conclusion was published in October 2018 as the *2019 Sustainability and Public Benefit Strategy*. This strategy recognises the ultimate importance of being sustainable and providing public benefit in all our outcomes.

Ben Uri today is committed to developing its two distinct operating divisions: firstly, the Ben Uri Research Unit (BURU), which is charged with developing Britain's first online digital resource recording the immigrant contribution to British visual culture since 1900 and including artists, scholars, critics, publishers, teachers, patrons and dealers. This consolidates, formalises and expands the museum's academic and ongoing focus on Jewish émigré artists, first launched in 2003, and expanded in 2011 via the Eva Frankfurther Research and Curatorial Fellowship for the Study of Émigré Artists. BURU will also continue to both streamline and qualitatively improve the collection through new acquisition and loan policies and to present short, sharp scholarly exhibitions, such as this one, as one of its research outcomes.

Secondly, the Ben Uri Arts and Dementia Unit (BUAD) is charged with further developing our eleven-year engagement with the elderly and those living with dementia into the country's first fully researched set of art interventions, using our collection as a resource.

These are exciting times for Ben Uri, as we craft new museum operating strategies to allow small scholarly-based institutions like our own to survive, prosper and deliver distinctive public benefit inspired by our heritage and collections.

David J Glasser
Chairman

Czech Routes/Roots: Variations on a Theme

"In London, I painted Prague again from memory, and called the painting Nostalgia*"*

Oskar Kokoschka

"We talked ... of the Czech and Moravian folk dances and customs which Feigl so loved and often painted in London – nostalgic memories of the past. He hummed one of the melancholy tunes, he looked in the large room where we were sitting at a picture of Prague with the Charles bridge connecting the little side of the town with the Altstadt"

J. P. Hodin

Long since Shakespeare endowed her in *The Winter's Tale* with 'deserts' and a 'sea-coast', 'fair Bohemia', the westernmost and largest historical region of the Czech lands, has been the subject of much mythologising, misinformation and misunderstanding. Indeed, in September 1938, despite being headline news, to the British, Czechoslovakia was at once an exotic and unknown entity. Due in part to a degree of geographical as well as cultural insularity, combined with a centuries old ambivalence towards continental Europe, in a BBC broadcast Prime Minister Neville Chamberlain declared: 'How horrible, fantastic, incredible, it is that we should be digging trenches and trying on gas-masks here because of a quarrel in a far-away country between people of whom we know nothing!' And yet, as early as the fourteenth century, it had been recognised that he who

ruled Bohemia effectively controlled the crossroads of Central Europe and the strategic importance of this beautiful and ancient territory has been the cause of many of the more turbulent chapters in her history.[2]

Czechoslovakia was founded in October 1918 as one of the central European successor states of the Austro-Hungarian Empire at the end of the First World War. Consisting of Bohemia, Moravia, Slovakia and Carpathian Ruthenia, it was a multi-ethnic state with Czechs and Slovaks as constituent peoples. Democracy thrived during the interwar period, so much so that of all the newly established Central European states, only Czechoslovakia preserved a democratic government until the outbreak of the Second World War.

In the wake of the Munich Conference which resulted in the cession of the Sudetenland to Germany, Chamberlain announced: '[...] for the second time in history, a British Prime Minister has returned from Germany bringing peace with honour. I believe it is peace in our time.' Far from sated, however, by such an outrageous act of piracy, Hitler had been emboldened and on 1st September 1939 war began. Nazi occupation of 'rump' Czechoslovakia resulted in mass displacement and by December 1939 some 12,000 refugees from Czechoslovakia were resident in Britain, a figure comprising 6,000 Czechoslovaks, 3,000 Sudeten Germans, 300 other Czech minorities, 1,000 Reich Germans, 800 Austrians and 800 unclassified individuals.[3] Of those registered with the Czech Refugee Trust Fund (formerly the British Committee for Refugees from Czechoslovakia) – a voluntary charitable organisation responsible for 'refugees whose prominence in opposition to Nazism and Fascism had brought their liberty and even their lives into danger', and who therefore needed 'to be rescued' – approximately 67% were Jewish, while more than half were 'wholly dependent upon the Trust for financial support' and not allowed to work. One of the many problems to confront the Trust was how to adapt a scheme for short term assistance that had not envisaged accommodating and maintaining refugees for an indefinite period, and certainly not in such large numbers. A solution lay in the hostel system which was more economical than private accommodation. There were seventeen directly controlled hostels at the commencement of the Trust and a further twenty-two were opened in the period to March 1940. These were located largely in London but also as far afield as Wales and Inverness in order to disperse the refugees.[4] Despite the fact that, as Jana Burešová notes, "some refugees did not readily adjust to hostel life with its shared, often overcrowded rooms, domestic duties and emphasis on self-sufficiency in order to supplement the 10 shillings which the Trust sent weekly to hostel wardens for every maintained resident", the majority were co-operative and supportive.[5]

Following its forced division and partial incorporation into Nazi Germany, the Czechoslovak state did not *de facto* exist and Britain became the centre of the Czechoslovak resistance movement abroad, hosting President Beneš and the Czechoslovak Government in Exile between 1940 and 1945. Chamberlain's shocking pronouncement revealed that despite being headline news, little was known about Czechoslovakia's cultural heritage. Patriotic exiles in Britain determined to remedy this through the activities of multi-faceted entities including social and cultural organisations such as the Czechoslovak Institute. Established at President Beneš's behest and formally opened by Anthony Eden, Secretary of State for Foreign Affairs, in January 1941, the Institute was designed to showcase Czechoslovak culture and was responsible for exhibiting the work of several of the artists represented in *Czech Routes* including Bedřich Feigl, Oskar Kokoschka, Freda Salvendy and Geza Szobel, before closing in 1948 following Czechoslovakia's Communist coup. The Institute frequently co-operated not only with the Anglo-Sudeten Club, conceived as "a cultural, social and political meeting place" for those of Sudeten origin and members of the British public, but also with other exile organisations including the Austrian Centre, the Free German League of Culture and the Artists International Association, their members united both by "profession, and probably also [by] refugee status"[6]. The Czechoslovak-British Friendship Club along with the Czechoslovak Army's SOKOL branch and regional clubs also played a vital role.[7]

It is perhaps not as well-known as it should be that Czechs and Slovaks made a significant contribution to Britain's war effort. 3,500 Czechoslovak pilots, as well as soldiers of the Czechoslovak Brigade fighting in France who managed to escape after her fall, were stationed at Cholmondeley Park, where, in July 1940, the Czechoslovak forces in the UK were officially formed. Between 1940 and 1945 2,507 Czechs and Slovaks served in four squadrons, officially employed by the RAF, and a further 5,623 soldiers served in the Czechoslovak Brigade. Indeed, in 1940 Czechoslovak airmen represented, after the Commonwealth nations, the second largest national contribution (after the Poles) to the Allied Forces during the Battle of Britain. It is fitting therefore, that sculptor Franta Bělský, a number of whose works are included in *Czech Routes*, should have been commissioned to design a war memorial in Prague to the 544 Czechs and Slovaks killed serving with the

RAF during the war.[8] The 1st Czechoslovak Armoured Brigade, founded in 1943, was sent to France not long after the D-Day landings to besiege the 15,000 German soldiers remaining in Dunkirk. The brigade suffered heavy casualties during the siege and it was not until the 9th May 1945 that the German garrison finally surrendered to General Alois Liška.

Post-war, approximately 50% of the Czechoslovak refugees who had been admitted to Britain remained, many applying for naturalisation. Meanwhile pre-war Czechoslovakia was re-established with the exception of Subcarpathian Ruthenia, which was annexed by the Soviet Union and incorporated into the Ukrainian Soviet Socialist Republic. 90% of the ethnic German population was subsequently expelled leaving some 250,000 people, many married to Czechs, some anti-fascists and those required for post-war reconstructive work, resident in Czechoslovakia. From 1948 to 1990, Czechoslovakia was part of the Eastern Bloc and ruled by a Communist totalitarian regime. A period of political liberalisation in 1968, known as the Prague Spring, was forcibly ended when the Soviet Union, assisted by several other Warsaw Pact countries, invaded. In 1989 the Czechoslovaks peacefully deposed their government and, following the Velvet Revolution in 1993, the state was renamed the Czech and Slovak Federal Republic, consisting of two sovereign states, the Czech Republic (Czechia) and the Slovak Republic (Slovakia).

With the accession of both the Czech Republic and Slovakia to the European Union in May 2004, Czech and Slovak peoples gained the right to live and work in any of its member states. The Office for National Statistics estimates that 45,000 Czech-born immigrants were resident in the UK in 2013 while an estimated 60,000 to 90,000 Slovaks were living in the UK as of last year. It is interesting to note the preference of Czech born immigrants for north (as well as central) London, specifically Golders Green, Finchley and Highgate, as indicated by the 2001 census, as well as the presence of the Czech and Slovak Bar and Restaurant in West Hampstead, originally acquired in the late 1940s as a meeting place for Czech and Slovak immigrants, many of whom had fought alongside the Allied Forces during the war, located a mere stone's throw from Ben Uri's home on Boundary Road.

Czech Routes is the fourth in Ben Uri's series of exhibitions designed to highlight the contribution of émigré artists to Britain since 1900, succeeding previous exhibitions on German, Polish and Austrian artists (2017-18). Featuring the work of 21 painters, printmakers and sculptors, many of whom fled to Britain as racial and political refugees from National Socialism, *Czech Routes* marks the 80th anniversary of Hitler's invasion of "rump" Czechoslovakia on 15th March 1939 – the Sudetenland, Czechoslovakia's northern frontier, having already ceded to Germany under the Munich Agreement of 29th September 1938. The exhibition showcases works drawn primarily from the Ben Uri Collection alongside external loans from private collections, and previously unseen archival material, celebrating the contribution of selected Czechoslovak émigré artists to British culture and highlighting their experiences, impact and legacy.

While portraitist and pioneering printmaker, Emil Orlik made his first trip to Britain in 1898, the majority of Czechoslovak artists exhibited, including Franta Bělský, Jacob Bornfriend, Dorrit Epstein, Bedřich Feigl and Walter Trier, along with Austrian expressionist (and Czechoslovak citizen), Oskar Kokoschka, and German photomontagist, John Heartfield, made forced journeys to the UK immediately prior to the outbreak of the Second World War. These also include sculptor Anita Mandl and painter-printmaker Käthe Strenitz, just two of the 669 *Kindertransportees* rescued by British humanitarian Nicholas Winton. Also represented are works by subsequent generations of Czechoslovak artists including Irena Sedlecká, who fled her country's totalitarian Communist regime in the 1960s, as well as those who, between the 1970s and 1990s, have made the positive decision to immigrate to Britain to study and develop professionally, namely contemporary multidisciplinary artists Tereza Bušková, Mila Fürstová and Tereza Stehlikova.

The Ben Uri Collection, the most comprehensive and important repository of works by late 19th, 20th and 21st century immigrant artists in the U.K. and the international museum sector, includes more than thirty works by thirteen Czechoslovak artists – Yehuda Bacon, Edith Birkin, Naomi Blake, Jacob Bornfriend, Bedřich Feigl, Leo Haas, Walter Herz, Scarlet Nikolska, Emil Orlik, Freda Salvendy, Käthe Strenitz, Walter Trier and Shraga Weil – of which ten feature in *Czech Routes*. Indicative of the museum's eclectic history of acquisition via gifts as well as by direct purchase, the presence of such works in the collection is bound up too with Ben Uri's rich exhibition history. Works by Bornfriend, Trier, Feigl and Strenitz were included in Ben Uri Art Gallery's *Summer Exhibition of Paintings, Sculpture and*

Drawings by Contemporary Artists in 1944, while Salvendy's *Prague* was included in *Ben Uri Collection of Paintings, Sculpture and Drawings* exhibition in 1946. An exhibition of *Paintings by Walter Trier and Sculpture by Else Fraenkel and Erna Nonnenmacher* followed in 1947 with Feigl and Bornfriend, along with Frank Auerbach, Claude Rogers, Josef Herman and Archibald Ziegler, featuring in *Twelve Contemporary Artists* in 1958. Feigl was the subject too of solo exhibitions in 1959 and in 1964 (which included *The Restaurant*), in celebration of his 80th birthday while drawings, lithographs and etchings by Yehuda Bacon, referred to in this instance as an Israeli artist, were shown in 1957 and succeeded by an exhibition dedicated to Käthe Strenitz's paintings in 1961, and subsequently, by *Shraga Weil - Melitta Schiffer*, including *Variations on a Theme* (1957), the following year. The work of Leo Haas was represented in Ben Uri's 1967 exhibition, simply titled, *Graphics* while in 1974 *Graphics by Jacob Bornfriend and Alfred Harris* was mounted at the gallery's Dean Street premises. The latter included Bornfriend's *Prague* Series - based on work he was forced to leave behind in 1939 when he fled to England from Czechoslovakia, as well as his *Jewish Festival* works, based on studies for the mural he painted for the library of Jews' College, London, now in the Ben Uri Collection. In 1975, the year after Scarlet Nikolska immigrated to Great Britain, the Ben Uri Art Gallery held a solo exhibition of her work, while in 1998 *Czech Jewish Artists from the Collection* featured her *Sabbath in Prague* painting along with Walter Herz's *Samson* (1947) and Emil Orlik's *Head of a Man*. This rich history is something that *Czech Routes* has sought both to highlight and to build upon

while the museum continues to augment its collection with the objective of assembling the UK's most comprehensive anthology of representative works by immigrant artists to Britain since 1900, in parallel with the work of the Ben Uri Research Unit.

In an article on the subject of 'The Visual Arts and Judaism', celebrated Czechoslovak art historian J.P. Hodin quotes Jacob Bornfriend's inquisitive response to the question 'as to whether the Jewish type as a stylistic feature also represents an element of Jewish art': 'Is there a Czech style, an English style, a Polish style?'[9] A rhetorical question of sorts, Bornfriend's retort reveals a distinct ambivalence towards generalisation and classification by creed or country. Without wishing to tackle the subject of a 'Czech style' at present, it is possible, however, to identify in a number of the works explored, nostalgia for a distant homeland as well as evocations of particular kinds of mourning and melancholia. These include Freda Salvendy's *Prague* (1947), a depiction of the Czechoslovak capital in a soft wash of muted watercolours, Scarlet Nikolska's *Sabbath in Prague*, indicative of a kind of affectionate piety for a vanished world rendered in ochres, and browns enlivened by white, yellow and blue and Bedřich Feigl's equally engrossing, *The Restaurant*. Inspired by the Slavonic atmosphere of the Czechoslovak capital and reminiscent too of his Berlin days, Feigl returned repeatedly to the motif of coffee houses and restaurants, which he referred to as 'the marketplaces of life'. Attempting to recreate continental 'kaffe haus' culture in London, Feigl and others gathered at Cosmo, West Hampstead, perhaps the subject of *The Restaurant*, where one could 'spend all day reading [...] over a single cup of coffee or consuming Schnitzel and Strudel with fellow refugees'.[10]

Nostalgia is evident too in the work of contemporary artists Tereza Bušková , Mila Fürstová and Tereza Stehliková. Bušková seeks in her practice to celebrate and reinterpret Slavic as well as European rituals through the media of print, performance and video. A series of three prints, produced as if they were postcards of the mythical town of *Erdingtonia* (2016), commemorate the clipping of the church - an ancient and almost forgotten English tradition as part of which families would flock to local churches, holding hands with each other in order to encircle it with open arms - by combining English customs with Bohemian wedding celebrations. Fürstová's *Nest* (2011) and *Town Tree* (2012) examine 'universal and personal mythologies'. In the artist's own words, the technique of etching reflects and informs the spirit of her work, for as the image "quietly grow[s]...a fragile silver line emerges from a dark background as if a distant memory was traced from the unconscious". Both *Nest* and *Town Tree*, in its depiction, perhaps, of Fürstová's Czech roots, also resonate with the themes of identity, migration and belonging. Similarly, in exploring how moving images can be used to capture and communicate both multi-sensory experiences and embodied memory, Stehliková too enters into a cross-disciplinary dialogue with her contemporaries. Her photographs which illustrate *Railtracks* (2013), a collaboration between writers John Berger and Anne Michaels, chart an elegiac, introspective and palpably atmospheric journey by train through the wintry landscapes of Southern Bohemia. Characterised by their liminality, as well as by their haunting beauty, in evading

exact periodisation such images function as mythic histories unbound by time.

The exhibition is notable too for the inclusion of works which evidence the awe-inspiring stoicism of their makers, as well as the indefatigable and inextinguishable capacity of the human spirit to endure. Such works include *Ghetto* (1945/66) and *Life, The Market Place* (1945/66), two of ten works by Leo Haas in the Ben Uri Collection printed after the war using the original plate, which had been created while the artist was imprisoned in Terezín ghetto, north of Prague, as well as *Outside the Prison* (1942) by Geza Szobel, Fernand Léger's former pupil, and subsequently, a soldier in the Czechoslovak Army in France. Expressed through the use of contrastingly light hearted, convivial subject matter the same spirit is also evident in Franta Bělský's *Joy-Ride* (1958), Jacob Bornfriend's *Blue Grey Fishes* (1960), Walter Trier's *Market Woman*, Oskar Kokoschka's *Still-Life Studio Exercise* (c. 1950) and *The Donkey*. It is likewise manifest in Dorrit Dekk's infectiously exuberant '*To Tasha*' (2010) and in Holocaust survivor, Yehuda Bacon's *Variations on a Theme* (1957), a unique and uncharacteristic celebration of form and colour. Whether forced or free, the routes these Czech-born artists took to Britain, as well as the roots they then set down, deserve to be far better known, for, as this exhibition and accompanying publication have served to illustrate, their presence and their practice in this country have significantly enriched British art and culture and continue to do so today.

Nicola Baird

Notes

1   Oskar Kokoschka cited Agnes Tieze, ed., *Oskar Kokoschka and the Prague Cultural Scene* (Köln: Wienand Verlag, 2016)

2   Peter Cannon-Brookes, *Czech Sculpture 1800-1938* (London: Trefoil Books, 1983)

3   Jana Barbora Burešová, 'The Czech Refugee Trust Fund in Britain 1939-50', in *Exile in and from Czechoslovakia during the 1930s and 1940s*, ed. by Charmian Brinson (Amsterdam: Rodopi, 2009)

4   Ibid.

5   Ibid.

6   The Anglo-Sudeten Club and the Czechoslovak Institute generally hosted separate social and cultural activities, The Anglo-Sudeten Club published a newspaper but did not organise exhibitions whereas the Czechoslovak Institute organised exhibitions but had no newspaper.

7   Jana Barbora Burešová, *London's Czechoslovak Institute during World War II*, Unpublished lecture, Research Centre for German and Austrian Exile Studies, Institute for Modern Languages Research, University of London. Lecture, 27th March 2019.

8   The abstract memorial, 14ft high and based on aerofoils, was unveiled by President Vaclav Havel in Prague, on 8th May 1995, the 50th anniversary of Czechoslovakia's liberation.

9   J.P. Hodin, 'The Visual Arts and Judaism', *Art Journal*, Vol. 23, No. 3 (Spring, 1964)

10 Daniel Snowman, *The Hitler Émigrés: The Cultural Impact on Britain of Refugees from Nazism* (London: Chatto & Windus, 2002, p.227)

Three Czechoslovak-born Sculptors

Brought together at the Czechoslovak Embassy in London in 1992, the life experiences of these three Czechoslovak-born sculptors could hardly be more different. Franta Bělský and Irena Sedlecká are both the product of formal art training in Prague and London, while Anita Mandl came to sculpture by way of zoology and an intimate knowledge of the anatomy of animals. Both Franta Bělský and Irena Sedlecká liked to stress, in conversation, the importance to them of the underlying facial bone structures of their subjects, and how the subtle distortions responding to the facial muscles conveyed the inner character of the sitter. This is part of the basic discipline instilled by the Academy in Prague, while Anita Mandl comes to a comparable synthesis by a different route, that of rigorous scientific research.

Franta Bělský

Franta Bělský, son of the eminent Jewish economist, Joseph Bělský, was born in Brno (6 April 1921), moving with his family to Prague as a small child. His middle-class academic upbringing encouraged the development of an independence of thought, and an early conviction as to the rightness of the conclusions he reached, which were characteristic of the internationalist intellectual milieu of Prague to which he belonged by reason of his family background. His father was, perhaps not surprisingly, not keen on the artistic aspirations of young Franta, even when he won first prize in a student sculpture competition aged sixteen.

Nonetheless, in 1938, he was prevailed upon to allow Franta to be admitted to a commercial art school in Prague, only to be overtaken by the German occupation of Bohemia and Moravia six months later. The family fled to England, and Franta re-started his studies, at the Central School of Arts & Crafts in London from which he won a place at the Royal College of Art.

The Second World War broke out in September 1939 and young Franta immediately enlisted with the Czech units which were beginning to be formed in England. His was sent to France in May 1940, but with the collapse of French resistance the unit made its way south and, via Gibraltar, returned to England a month after Dunkirk. The Czech units gathered in Cholmondeley Park, Cheshire, where they were reviewed by Winston Churchill. Franta records scrutinising the Prime Minister closely and resolving, when the time came, to sculpt him as he had seen him that day. During the years before preparations for the Normandy Invasion, Franta was sent by the Czech Army to continue his studies for two terms at the Royal College of Art under Richard Garbe. In 1943 he exhibited *Weasel* at The Royal of Arts, which he had carved from Jarra Wood carried round in his kitbag. It was then that he met Margaret Owen who he married shortly before leaving for Normandy. Initially serving as a gunner under Montgomery, he transferred to the American Army, serving under Patton, and ended the War in Czechoslovakia.

Joined by Margaret, they set up home in

Prague where he recommended his studies, now at the Academy of Fine Arts under the relief sculptor Otakar Spaniel. From this period dates the *Paratroop Memorial* which he executed in Spaniel's studio in 1947 and the uniface *Zátopek Medal* commissioned by the Czech Army in 1948. With the communist takeover of Czechoslovakia that same year, Franta and Margaret hurriedly returned to London where he resumed his studies at the Royal College, this time under Frank Dobson and John Skeaping. Before graduating, Franta exhibited his posthumous portrait of *Jan Masarik* at the Royal Academy, in 1949, and, in 1950, that of *Lt. Col. Peniakoff* (Popski) who had become a personal friend. The Festival of Britain offered both potential work and the opportunity of seeing the creations of a wide range of British sculptors, not least new ideas for fountains. His over-life-size bronze figure of *Cecil Rhodes* executed in 1953 for Bulawayo and unveiled by HM The Queen demonstrated clearly his skill at an early age for tackling monumental figures, but it attracted little attention in Britain.

Rather more attention was directed towards the newly-founded Society of Portrait Sculptors and its exhibition *Personalities in Sculpture* displayed in Edinburgh, August-September 1954, and subsequently at the Imperial Institute Gallery, South Kensington, to which Franta contributed his portrait of *Peniakoff*. With *Lesson*, executed for the London County Council in 1955 and *Joy-Ride* for Stevenage New Town Centre (1958), Franta established a strong position to satisfy the admittedly waning demand by local government patrons for monumental figurative compositions. Concurrently, however, he was also developing entirely abstract forms

for fountains, above all the monumental composition created for the European Shell Centre, South Bank, completed in 1961. In all his compositions Franta was determinedly anti-elitist with a deep belief in what he termed the "social" role of his sculpture. Not surprisingly, his aversion to the art market, and what he saw as its pernicious influence on artists, expressed with uncomfortable clarity and certainty could be interpreted as arrogance, and relations with the Royal Academy became increasingly difficult.

Nonetheless, Franta's excellent rapport with his portrait sitters is borne out by the portrait sculptures from life which he executed of four generations of the Royal Family and his selection for a sequence of highly prestigious naval portraits culminating in the more than 9 foot bronze figure of *Earl Mountbatten* overlooking Horse Guards Parade (1983). The opportunity to work up his memories of Winston Churchill in 1940 came to fruition with the commission by Westminster College, Fulton, Missouri, for an over-life-size bronze figure close to the spot where Churchill had delivered his 'Iron Curtain' speech. Unveiled in 1971, Franta developed something of a line in sculpted portraits of the wartime leader, much to the irritation of Lady Churchill, culminating in the half-length figures outside the British Embassy in Prague (1992) which she declined to unveil.

The Society of Portrait Sculptors went into hibernation in 1984, but was revived by Franta and others in 1996, with Franta as its President. Margaret had died in 1989, and the ever closer relationship with his fellow student from Prague, Irena Sedlecká, led to their marriage in 1985. Active in his Studio almost to the end, Franta died 5th July 2000.

Irena Sedlecká

Visitors to London, walking down Jermyn Street in St. James's, will encounter the elegant figure of Beau Brummel facing the Piccadilly Arcade. Relatively few, however, realise that the over-life-size bronze figure was executed by Irena Sedlecká, the most distinguished Czech-born figurative sculptor working in Britain today.

A native of Pilsen in South-Western Czechoslovakia, as it was then, Irena Sedlecká began her artistic training as a seventeen-year-old student at the Academy in Prague when it re-opened after the end of the Second World War. Her Professor of Sculpture, Karel Pokorný, ensured that during the ensuing six years she received a very thorough grounding in the artistic and technical aspects of figurative sculpture. The Communist takeover in 1948 provided plentiful public commissions for sculptors and, at least at first, an enhanced status for creative artists. Prestigious commissions for monumental sculpture were forthcoming and a brilliant career beckoned, with all-expenses-paid holidays on the Black Sea, but they failed to retain her, and, in 1966, she succeeded in travelling, via Yugoslavia, with her three children, to London.

The period 1967-1974 was in her own words 'Wasted Years' during which she made little sculpture, but the practical training which she had received in Prague enabled her to earn a modest living doing occasional sculptural modelling jobs for the British Museum and others. She first exhibited with the Society of Portrait Sculptors, in London, in 1967, but her big breakthrough was not until 1978, the result of the success of the commission for the *Head of Sir Laurence Olivier*. This led to the commission for the over-life-size bronze figure of *Freddie Mercury* for Montreux which is best known to Londoners as the original of the enlarged version in fibre-glass which ornamented for many years the canopy of the theatre at the south end of Tottenham Court Road.

Notwithstanding her modest dismissal of her own work, and her generosity in respect of the works of her competitors, the long series of portrait heads which Irena Sedlecká has exhibited at the Annual Exhibitions of the Society of Portrait Sculptors from 1974 have maintained an extremely high standard, attracting a galaxy of distinguished sitters. Many of her earlier subjects were from the world of the performing arts, with impressive heads of the actors *James Berwick* (exhibited 1979), *Laurence Olivier* (as Hamlet, 1980), *Kenneth Williams* (1981), *Donald Sinden* (as Othello, 1982), *Paul Bacon* (1982), *Paul Eddington* (1984) and *Nigel Hawthorn* (1984), as well as the eloquent small-scale seated figure of *John Gielgud* (as Hamlet), arguably the most successful model in her series of statuettes of actors. All of this has been achieved during decades when the figurative tradition in Britain has been under assault from Modernism and received scant encouragement from the Contemporary Art elite or state organisations, including the National Portrait Gallery. The reinvigoration, in recent years, of the figurative tradition in public esteem owes much to Irena Sedlecká and her third husband, the Czech-born sculptor Franta Bělský, who have been superb ambassadors for sculpture, inspiring total confidence in artists and patrons alike.

In more recent years, Irena Sedlecká acquired her most important patron, the eccentric publisher Felix Dennis.

For his personal Valhalla on his estate in Warwickshire, populated by bronze statues of his heroes and heroines, she executed the remarkable over-life-size seated figure of Sir Arthur Conan Doyle behind whom rises the phantasmagoric figure of Sherlock Holmes. Her second over-life-size bronze sculpture for Felix Dennis represents the American poetess Emily Dickinson, which was particularly problematic to achieve because no profile image of her is known. The programme of commissions put in hand by Felix Dennis is conspicuous for its idiosyncrasies, but it is nevertheless by a wide margin the most important programme of figurative sculpture to be undertaken in Britain since the Second World War. Consequently, it is profoundly to be hoped that in due course both of Irena Sedlecká's sculptures, and their companions, will become more easily accessible to the British public.

Anita Mandl

Anita Mandl was born in Prague in 1927, the daughter of the Jewish owner of a paper-mill situated near Karlovy Vary. While Anita was sent to London on one of the last 'Kindertransport' together with her sixteen-year-old brother, her father died not long after the German occupation of Bohemia and Moravia, and her mother, a talented pianist, was deported to Terezín and did not survive the Holocaust. On arrival in England, Anita's guardian was Anne Stephens, a Quaker schoolmistress in London where she began her English education. She was soon transferred to the care of one of her sisters, Mrs. Rogers, in Dudley, where she went to school with her daughters at Dudley Girls' High School. Anita remained there until the summer of 1942

when, having passed School Certificate, her biology mistress encouraged her to move to London, if she could, and aim for a University of London degree via Birkbeck College.

Lacking family support, she was anxious to become financially independent as soon as possible and quickly obtained basic secretarial training so as to be able to earn some money while studying in the evenings at Birkbeck. She obtained a General B.Sc. in 1945 and stayed on at Birkbeck, taking an Honours Degree in Zoology in 1946. She left her secretarial job and became a Research Assistant at the Royal London Hospital. After a year she was offered a job by Professor Solly Zuckerman in the Anatomy Department of Birmingham University. There she obtained her Ph.D. in 1951 and D.Sc. in 1960 while attending evening classes in sculpture at the Birmingham College of Art.

Her first wood-carving, in mahogany, was completed in 1955 at the College of Art, Margaret Street, where her teacher was Bill Daley. It was he who encouraged Anita to persevere with sculpture and during this time she executed a number of portraits. The summer schools at Attingham Park in Shropshire, entitled 'creative leisure', provided enhanced spiritual energy. Able to immerse herself in carving, Anita spent several holidays there, equipped with her blocks of wood or alabaster. Under the benevolent aegis of Sir George Trevelyan, Bart., lodging and food were provided, thereby letting pupils work undisturbed from breakfast until bed-time in any artistic medium they liked. Trevelyan, a committed Quaker and often described as "a New Age spiritual thinker", was appointed Warden of the pioneering adult education college established at Attingham Park in 1948.

Despite the fact that both Shropshire County Council and the University of Birmingham, Attingham's joint sponsors, expressed misgivings about his promulgation of spiritual knowledge in the context of adult education in an increasingly strident, materialistic world, Trevelyan remained the driving force at Attingham until his retirement in 1971.

In 1965 Anita married, resigned her University Readership, and moved with her husband to Devon. There she established a studio and began her contributions to the long series of exhibitions featuring her animal sculptures starting at the Royal West of England Academy, Bristol, of which she was elected Associate in 1967. Her *Owl,* carved from beautifully figured Rio Rosewood in 1969, has a moving inner tranquillity which echoes her formation as a sculptor and sets it aside from the proliferation of animal carvings and exotically patinated bronzes now so popular. Supplies of appropriate tropical hardwoods became increasingly scarce by the 1970s and so she turned to other species of wood, alabaster and marble for the creation of her animal sculptures. Economic necessity encouraged Anita in due course to look to bronze editions of her carved animal sculptures, and this has led to a long partnership with the Pangolin foundry and Rungwe Kingdon who have developed some of the most colourful surface finishes now available.

In 1978 Anita became a full Member of the Royal West of England Academy and two years later a Fellow of the Royal Society of British Sculptors. She has exhibited seven times in the Summer Exhibitions of the Royal Academy of Arts, London, and in May 1992 joined Franta Bělský and Irena Sedlecká in exhibiting a group of her animal sculptures as part of *Czech and Slovak Sculpture in Great Britain* at the Czechoslovak Embassy in London. Today, aged ninety-one, Anita Mandl continues to live and work in Devon.

Peter Cannon-Brookes

Chronologies

Franta Bělský

1921 Born Brno, 6 April, son of Jewish economist, Joseph Bělský

Childhood in Prague

1938 Aged 17 admitted to a commercial art school in Prague

German Occupation of Czechoslovakia

Bělský family left Prague for London

Franta enrolled at the Central School of Arts & Crafts, London, and won place at Royal College of Art

1939 September, outbreak of Second World War

Enlisted in Czechoslovak Army units in Britain

1940 Sent to France with his unit

After the Fall of France, returned to Britain via South of France

1943-44 "Standing and Waiting": two terms at The Royal College of Art, under Richard Garbe

1943 *Weasel* carved from Jarra Wood exhibited at Royal Academy

1944 Married Margaret Owen before departure for D Day Normandy Landings

1945 Ended World War II in Czechoslovakia serving last three months with U.S. Army under Patten

Joined in Prague by Margaret

1945-48 Studied at the Academy of Fine Arts, Prague, in Sculpture School under Otakar Spaniel

1947 *Paratroop Memorial*, Prague, executed in Spaniel's studio

1948 *Zátopek Medal*

Communist takeover of Czechoslovakia

Returned to London and resumed studies at The Royal College of Art, under Frank Dobson and John Skeaping

1949 *Jan Masarik* portrait exhibited at The Royal Academy

1950 *Doorknocker, and Lt. Col. Peniakoff (Popski)* exhibited at The Royal Academy

A.R.C.A. Hons. Dip., 1st Class, awarded by The Royal College of Art

1952 Festival of Britain

Constellation, and portraits of *Peter Ustinov and Cecil Day Lewis*

1953 *Cecil Rhodes* for Bulawayo, *Constellation*, Colchester

1954 Personalities in Sculpture exhibition in Edinburgh organised by the Society of Portrait Sculptors, and the Imperial Institute Gallery, South Kensington

1954-55 Statuette of Winston Churchill, *"1940" 197Study* exhibited

1955 *Lesson*, for London County Council, Bethnal Green

Girl, Jill Balcon

1956 *Miss Susan Whittet*

1958 *Triga*, Caltex House, Knightsbridge

Joy Ride, Stevenage New Town Centre

1959 October, '56 Society Exhibition, Birmingham University, *Franta Bělský*

1960 *Aerial Form, Sir Arthur Thomson, Sleeping Centaur*

1961 Fountain for European Shell Centre, South Bank, completed

1962 *HM Queen Elizabeth The Queen Mother* for Birmingham University

Caroline Hewatt

1963 *HRH The Prince Andrew 3 ½ Years Old*

Caroline Hewatt

1963-68 President of the Society of Portrait Sculptors

1965 Awarded the Jean Masson Davidson International Award for Portrait Sculpture

1969 *Admiral Cunningham*, Trafalgar Square

Sherban Cantacuzino

Astronomer Herschel Memorial, Slough

1971 *Winston Churchill*, Churchill Memorial and Library, Fulton, Missouri

1971 *Winston Churchill*, bust in Churchill Archives, Cambridge

1972 *Winston Churchill*, relief for P&O, *The Spirit of London*

Chief Odutola

President Harry S Truman, bust for Presidential Library, Independence, Missouri

1975 *Totem*, Manchester Arndale Centre, and awarded the Royal Society of British Sculptors' *Sir Otto Beit Medal* in respect of it 1976

Oracle, Temple Way House, Bristol

1976 *Lord Cottesloe*, National Theatre

Royal Society of British Sculptors' *Sir Otto Beit Medal*

1978 *John Dutton, Lord Chandos*

Royal Society of British Sculptors' *Sir Otto Beit Medal*

Jean Masson Davidson Award for Distinction in Portrait Sculpture

1979 *HRH The Prince Philip, Duke of Edinburgh*, National Portrait Gallery, London

Sir John Methven

President Harry S. Truman, Truman Dam, Osage River, Missouri

1980 *Crown Coin*, Queen Mother 80th Birthday, Guernsey issue

1981 *HM The Queen*, National Portrait Gallery, London

Sally Korda

1982 *Duet, Passacaglia*

1983 *Earl Mountbatten*, monument, Horse Guards Parade

1984 *HRH The Prince Andrew*, National Portrait Gallery, London

Society of Portrait Sculptors goes into hibernation (until 1986)

1985 *HRH The Prince William, Admiral of the Fleet Lord Lewin*, HMS Dryad

1986 *HM The Queen*, Queen Elizabeth II Conference Centre, Westminster

1987 *John Piper*

1988 *Leap* fountain, Blackwall Basin

1989 Death of Margaret Bělský

1980 *Chanticleer*, for Rank Xerox

1982 *Winston Churchill*, bust for Prague

Czech & Slovak Sculptors in Great Britain exhibition at the Czechoslovak Embassy, London

Monograph *Franta Bělský – sculpture* published

1985 Prague Memorial to Czechoslovaks who served with the RAF

1986 Society of Portrait Sculptors revived with Franta Bělský as President

Married Irena Sedlecká

1987 *Mick Lunn*

Hon. Doctor of Fine Arts, Westminster College, Fulton, Missouri

1988 *Jorgen Jahre*

1989 *Wenceslas Hollar*, Southwark Cathedral

Awarded the Presidential Medal of Merit by Czech President, Václav Havel

2000 Died 5 July

Irena Sedlecká:

1928 Born in Pilsen

1938 German occupation of Czechoslovakia and closure of the Academy of Fine Arts, Prague

1944 Further education denied by German authorities and sent to work in a factory, until May 1945

1945 Pilsen liberated by the American Army

Started studies in the Academy of Fine Arts, Prague, in the Sculpture School under Karel Pokorný and V.V.Stech

1948 Communist takeover of Czechoslovakia

1949 Graduated from the Academy and awarded the State Prize for Excellence

1952 Lenin Museum competition won by Irena Sedlecká and Ludwig Kodym (married 1952)

1954 Klement Gottwald Mausoleum sculpture competition won by Sedlecká and Kodym

Four weeks holiday in Soviet Union included as part of the prize, spent in Sochy

1958 Divorced Kodym and married Stefan Drexler, a pediatrician who had served with Czech units in the British army

1950s *Monument to the Victims of the Nazi Regime*, Velke Mezirice, Moravia

Monument to Julius Fucik, Pilsen

1965 *God is Dead* receives official approval

1966 Arrival in London (September) with Drexel and three children

1967 Exhibited at the Society of Portrait Sculptors, *Franz Kafka*

1967-74 The 'Wasted Years' occasional modelling jobs for David Perrot and British Museum

1970 Separated from Stefan Drexler

1974 – Exhibited regularly with the Society of Portrait Sculptors

1978 *Head of Laurence Olivier, Arnold Schonberg, Raymond Baxter*

1980 *Sir Laurence Olivier as Oedipus, Ted Moult, Kenneth Kendall*

1981 'Talking Heads' Project and giant head of *Laurence Olivier*

Donald Sinden as Othello, Jackie Stewart

1983 *Lord Lichfield, Magnus Magnusson*

1984 *Benjamin Britten, Nigel Hawthorn, Paul Eddington*

Society of Portrait Sculptors goes into hibernation (until 1986)

1985 *Sir Laurence Olivier* (the last portrait of him taken from life)

Maria Callas

1986 *Maria Callas as Violetta*

1989 Death of Margaret Bělský

1987 *Sir Frank Whittle, Baudelaire*

1988 *Maria Callas as Norma, Johannes Brahms*

1981 Death of Freddie Mercury from AIDS

Bust of Freddie Mercury and commission to proceed with large-scale bronze

Lawrence Olivier as Mr. Puff

1982 Exhibition *Czech & Slovak Sculptors in Great Britain*, at Czechoslovak Embassy, London, May

Paul Scofield as Salieri, Joan Sutherland as Lucia di Lammermoor

1983 *John Gielgud as Richard II, John Gielgud as Hamlet*

1984 *Ralph Richardson as Falstaff, Beau Brummel* maquette

1986 *Franta Bělský, Freddie Mercury* installed in Montreux

Society of Portrait Sculptors revived with Franta Bělský as President

Married Franta Bělský as third husband

1988 *Architect Josef Svoboda* for National Theatre, Prague

1989 *Emmy Destinn197The Diva* installed at Straz nad Nezarkou

2000 Death of Franta Bělský

2001 *Conan Doyle and Sherlock Holmes* installed on the estate of Felix Dennis

2004 *Paula Fenwick*

Awarded the Jean Masson Davidson Medal

2007 *Emily Dickinson* installed on the estate of Felix Dennis

2010 *Jan Hruška*

2011 *The Meeting at the Cabaret Lapin Agile, Paris*

2016 Left Sutton Courtney for a care home near London

Anita Mandl:

1926 17 May, born in Prague, daughter of Dr. Bohumir Mandl, proprietor of a paper mill near Karlsbad, and early education in Prague. Mother a talented pianist who taught Anita.

1939 Came to London on one of the last *kindertransport* together with her brother aged almost 16, and began English education.

1 September Operation Pied Piper and evacuation of children from London begun.

9 September Declaration of War against Germany and beginning of Second World War.

Anita transferred to Dudley, West Midlands.

1940-42 Educated at Dudley Girls High School and passed School Certificate.

1942 Summer, left Dudley for London and crash course at a secretarial college, leading to a secretarial job, and began studying in the evenings at Birkbeck College, University of London.

1945 Awarded a General B.Sc., University of London, Birkbeck College.

1946 Awarded Honours Degree in Zoology, University of London, Birkbeck College.

Left secretarial job and took up post as a Research Assistant at Royal London Hospital.

1947 Recruited by Professor Solly Zuckerman for the Department of Anatomy, Medical School, Birmingham University,

1951 Awarded Ph.D. in Zoology, Birmingham University, while attending evening classes in sculpture at Birmingham College of Art.

1955 First wood carving, in mahogany, completed under the guidance of Bill Daley.

1957 October'56 Society Exhibition of sculpture shown in Birmingham University, including work by Franta Bělský.

1960 Awarded D.Sc. in Zoology, Birmingham University, and attended Summer Schools at Attingham Park over a number of years.

Bust of Sir Arthur Thomson, by Franta Bělský, unveiled in Birmingham University.

1965 Married Dr. Denys Jennings, resigned her Readership, and moved to Budleigh Salterton, Devon.

Began construction of studio and collecting materials for sculpture, the process taking two Years.

1967 Exhibited at Royal West of England Academy, Bristol, and elected Associate Member.

1969 26 November, *Owl 1*, carved from Rio Rosewood, completed.

1971 Elected Sculpture Member of Royal Society of Marine Artists, but resigned in 1994.

1972 Elected Associate of the Royal Society of British Sculptors.

1976-88 Active as a Member of the Devon Guild of Craftsmen.

1978 Elected full Member of the Royal West of England Academy.

1979 Founder of the Otter Valley Association, an amenity society established to interest residents in the history, geography, wildlife and architecture of this area of Devon.

1980 Elected Fellow of the Royal Society of British Sculptors.

1987 Beginning of close association with Pangolin Editions casting in bronze editions of Anita Mandl's carved animal sculptures.

1982 May, with Franta Bělský and Irena Sedlecká contributed work to the exhibition *Czech and Slovak Sculpture in Great Britain* shown in the Czechoslovak Embassy in London.

2002 Commissioned by Pangolin Editions to execute sculpture for casting in silver for the *Sterling Stuff* collection of fifty sculptures in silver.

Friedrich Feigl: an artist whose life spanned the great upheavals of the 20th century

Friedrich Feigl (1884-1965) arrived in London in the summer of 1939, having fled German occupied Czechoslovakia, to join a large émigré community, many of whose members were Jewish. A painter, prolific printmaker and renowned illustrator, Feigl's reputation was then amongst the most recognised of living artists working in Central Europe.

Born in Prague into a German-speaking Jewish family, the third of six children, Feigl was brought up in the Old Town and witnessed the clearance of the Prague Ghetto. He showed an early interest in art and, in 1903, entered the Akademie Výtvarných Umění forming a strong friendship with a group of students who protested at the traditional curriculum. He left at the end of his second year, along with Bohumil Kubišta, and spent the next two years travelling abroad, at first with Otakar Kubin with whom he visited the Salon d'Automne in Paris where they saw Fauvist works by Derain and Matisse. In 1906 he made an extended tour of Europe with Antonin Procházka and Emil Filla visiting Croatia and Berlin where, in the Kunstsalon Cassirer, they first saw paintings by Cezanne. Feigl then made contact with Max Liebermann with whom he was often to be compared. The following year he - with his friends, Czech, German and Jewish from the Akademie - was instrumental in the organisation of an exhibition in Prague which caused a scandal due to the modernity of the paintings. This group of eight became well known as 'Osma'. Criticised by the Czech speaking nationalist community, support for Osma in Bohemia came mostly from the German-speaking Jewish community and writers such as Max Brod, through whom, most probably, he first met Franz Kafka. In a city increasingly dominated by Czech-language artistic and cultural institutions, however, there were fewer opportunities for German-speaking artists to exhibit and Feigl's work reveals that, unlike many of his contemporaries, he chose not to pursue cubism or abstraction but to develop an art 'rooted in the world of nature and observed experience'.

By 1911, Feigl and his German wife Margarete were living in Berlin, but were continually in touch with Prague. The following year his contemporary, Franz Kafka, writing to his fiancé, told her "to go and meet the Feigls in their new home in Berlin to choose a painting for a wedding present and get to know the Feigls better". Berlin at this time was a melting pot for Modernist art and literature offering opportunities for artists not to be found elsewhere. Feigl continually sketched his friends, many of whom were Jewish, as they discussed their art and read their poems in cafés, bars and artists' salons. He painted landscapes and suburban Berlin street scenes which were to become the basis for albums of prints including *Fünfzehn lithographierte Landschaften von Friedrich*

Feigl, 1915 published by J.B.Neumann, one of Feigl's great supporters. Feigl also took part in exhibitions organised by Paul Cassirer, the great patron of the Berlin Secession, and soon concentrated on graphic art, which became an increasingly important part of his output. During the First World War he contributed illustrations to journals including *Kriegzeit,* edited by Paul Cassirer.

Early in 1918 he moved to Vienna and exhibited there with a new group of artists, which included Katharina Rapaport-Zirner, Freda Salvendy, and perhaps Adolf Loos. Known as the *Bewegung,* their work was close to the wider extremes of Expressionism. Almost unknown today, they nonetheless have their place in the story of Central European Modernism. His graphic work led to his exploration of his own identity as a Jewish artist and the Jewish subject matter which was central to his career. In 1919, he produced nine lithographs for the book *German Poets in Prague,* published by Oskar Wiener, and completed a series of twelve lithographs for *Prager Ghetto* in 1921. Feigl had a very personal connection with this subject matter given that his mother's family had lived in the Ghetto for generations and he himself had spent a substantial part of his childhood and youth there. These inspired the first monograph to be devoted to him, by George Marzinsky, a Jewish theorist and advocate of Expressionism, which in turn led

to his commission from the Berlin publisher Erich Reiss to provide illustrations for Balzac's *Gobseck.* The following year Feigl took part in the exhibition *Graphic Art by* Jewish Artists mounted at the Lucerna Palace. He continued meanwhile to exhibit in Prague including as part of the *Exhibition of 19th and 20th century Jewish Artists* held at the Fenix Palace on Wenceslas Square organised by his gallerist brother Hugo. Feigl was always concerned not to lose his intimate relationship with Prague but also not to remain a foreigner in each new homeland.

In 1933, with the growing power of the Nazis in Germany and increased anti-Semitism, Feigl and Margarete, like many others, decided to return to Prague. One document reveals that in Berlin, in late January 1933, he visited the Czech Consulate to acquire a passport which would allow him to go to Palestine to gather illustrations for an anthology of Prague Jewish stories. There he visited Jerusalem, Haifa, the Sea of Galilee and other sites collecting material and he returned with gouaches, water-colours and sketches. His illustrations were brought together in an anthology of Jewish stories published as *Die Goldene Gasse,* 1933. He also returned to oil painting, exploring themes connected with Jewish traditions in works including *The Tombstone of Mordechai Meisel,* 1932, and *Old-New Synagogue,* 1932-34, (both Jewish Museum, Prague). His last exhibition in

Prague was of thirty-four paintings of Palestine and Prague subjects held in 1937 at his brother's gallery, on the Masarykově Nábřeží.

In April 1939 Feigl and his wife left Prague by train to come to England but were arrested in Westphalia and briefly interned. Acting on advice from their friend Oskar Kokoschka, who was already in England, they sought help from the English Artists' Refugee Committee and the British Consulate in Cologne, and finally reached London. They were eventually to settle in a flat in Belsize Park with many immigrants as their neighbours, including the sculptress Elizabeth Wolff-Furth and the Czech art historian Dr Josef Hodin, who became a close friend. Feigl immediately threw himself into the artistic life of the London-based exiles, participating in the *First Group Exhibition of German, Austrian, Czechoslovakian Painters and Sculptors*, held at the Wertheim Gallery and sponsored by the newly established Free German League of Culture. As one of the four Czechoslovak painters, along with two sculptors, he exhibited two paintings, one of which depicts a view of *Tower Bridge,* thereby immediately associating himself with his new surroundings.

The Leicester Museum and Art Gallery, under the Directorship of Trevor Thomas, mounted a number of exhibitions devoted to British War artists as well as works by other nationalities including Czechs. At Feigl's instigation, in June 1941, the museum hosted the exhibition *Three Czechs: Bedrich Feigl, Freda Salvendy, Karel Vogel* and purchased four of Feigl's watercolour landscapes. He continued to paint lively scenes, not least watercolours of London park life in 'en plein air'. He returned too to depictions of people, many of whom were émigrés, in coffee

houses and restaurants which recalled those of his Berlin days. In 1944 the Czechoslovak Institute at 18 Grosvenor Place celebrated Feigl's 60th birthday with a solo exhibition of paintings produced since his arrival in England. The critical views were mixed, though T.W. Earp, of the *Daily Telegraph,* commended the assembled "recollected impressions of the artist's own and other countries". Feigl regularly contributed to exhibitions at the Ben Uri Art Gallery, London which purchased, in 1950, for its permanent collection, his large oil painting *View of Richmond.* This was displayed in the 'Art Section' curated by the Ben Uri Art Gallery which accompanied the *Anglo-Jewish Exhibition 1851-1951,* as part of the Festival of Britain celebrations. Feigl was given his first solo exhibition at the Ben Uri Art Gallery in 1959, comprising thirty-three oils and twelve watercolours, including views of the Thames near Richmond, portraits, café scenes and mythological subjects. Feigl was not only an exhibitor but was also involved with the Gallery over many years, playing an active role in its exhibitions programme.

A year before his death, in 1964 Feigl's 80th birthday was celebrated with a major exhibition at the Ben Uri Art Gallery of forty oils and fourteen watercolours executed in England. Reproduced on the cover of the catalogue was the portrait bust of the artist sculpted by Elizabeth Wolff-Furth while inside it featured an authoritative biography by J.P.Hodin, who described Feigl as "good conversationalist, a man of deep knowledge", with whom he would chat fondly of "the old days" as they sat smoking their pipes and looking at pictures of old Prague. On the occasion of the exhibition, he was interviewed by the *Jewish Chronicle* which congratulated him on his "steadfastness of vision and continued faith in the human figure as a proper subject for art". However, notwithstanding Feigl's efforts to integrate himself into the culture of his final homeland, his work remains unmistakably Central European and thus the victim of deeply rooted Anglo-Saxon prejudice. The British art establishment in the guise of its national institutions, not least the National Gallery, the Tate Gallery and the Arts Council, have always been lukewarm in their recognition of the qualities of Central European art, in part due to the chauvinism of their governing bodies reinforced by the experiences of two World Wars.

More recently Feigl has been the subject of an exhibition shown in Bohemia, at the Galerie Vtvarného Umění v Chebu, (2016), and the Alšova Jihočeská Galerie v Hluboké nad Vlatavou (2016-2017) and accompanied by an excellent publication, *Friedrich Feigl,* in German and Czech, edited by Nicholas Sawicki with contributions by Rachel Dickson, Sarah MacDougall, Arno Pařík and Zuzana Duchová to whom credit must be given for much of the information presented here.

Caroline Cannon-Brookes

Catalogue
of works
in exhibition
order

Freda Salvendy (Frieda)
(1887, Vienna, Austria-1968, Malvern, England)

Prague, 1947
Watercolour on paper
35.5 x 45.5 cm

Ben Uri Collection

Immigrated to Great Britain 1938

Painter and graphic artist, Freda Salvendy was born in Vienna (though her family originated from Neustadt an der Waag, now known as Néve Mésto nad Vahom, Slovakia), attending art school aged fifteen and later continuing her education in Frankfurt under the tutelage of artists Albin Egger-Lienz and Felix A. Harta. A founding member of the Bewegung ('Movement') along with Bedřich Feigl, an association of artists who advocated spirituality as the purpose of art as opposed to the decorative tendencies of Art Nouveau, she was also a member of the Wiener Frauenkunst ('Viennese Association of Female Artists and Craftswomen') and one of the few women to join the Hagenbund, an influential art association in post-First World War Vienna. As the Nazi threat increased, in 1938 Salvendy was forced to flee to England. Her artistic career in Britain was modest and although she exhibited in 1941 with the Artists International Association (AIA) and the Free German League of Culture (FGLC) as well as with Ben Uri in 1945 and 1946, since her death in 1968, her work has received little recognition. Her reputation, however, is currently undergoing a reassessment and in 2017 she featured in the Jewish Museum Vienna's survey show *Die Bessere Hälfte Jüdische Kunstlerinnen bis 1938* (The Better Half – Jewish Women Artists Before 1938) along with Margarete Berger-Hammerschlag, Bettina Ehrlich and Marie-Louise von Motesciszky. She is sometimes identified as a Czech artist and here depicts Prague in a soft wash of watercolours.

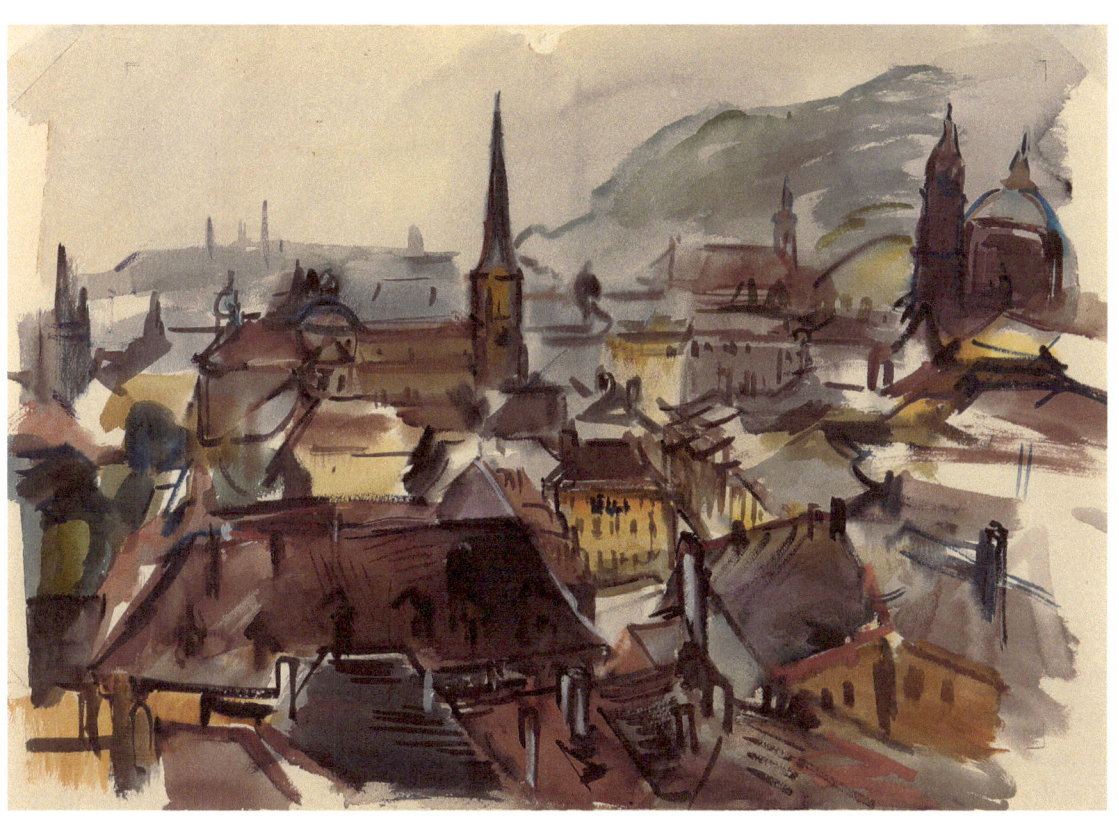

Käthe Strenitz

(1923, Gablonz, Bohemia- 2017, London, England)

Village

Watercolour on paper
39.5 x 51.5 cm

Ben Uri Collection

Immigrated to Great Britain 1939

Bohemian-born Käthe Strenitz studied in Prague at the Officina Pragensis under the tutelage of Hugo Steiner. At the age of 16 Strenitz was one of the 669 'Winton children', who in 1939 travelled on a Quaker-sponsored Kindertransport to England leaving her family behind in the Nazi occupied Sudetenland, Czechoslovakia's northern frontier. Following difficult experiences as a refugee including dairy and farm labour she arrived in London to find that Mrs Winton had sent some of her drawings to Austrian émigré artist Oskar Kokoschka, upon whose recommendation she was awarded a British Council scholarship at Regent Street Polytechnic. Dissatisfied with the teaching, however, she committed instead to war work making air force goggles, moving into a Czech Refugee Trust Fund-maintained hostel, where she met her future husband, Otto Fischel, a Czech-Jewish journalist-turned-entrepreneur whose plastics factory, south of the Old Caledonian Market, along with the surrounding industrial landscape- the railway tracks, tunnels and bridges of King's Cross- was to become the main subject of her work for almost 40 years. When she ventured away from King's Cross it was only to follow the Regent's Canal up to Camden Lock, to explore and sketch the back streets of Islington, or to find another rich source of industrial architecture amidst the riverside cranes and gantries of Rotherhithe and Bermondsey. Her fascination with such railway lands is attributed to her arrival as a *Kindertransportee* at London's Liverpool Street Station. In subsequent years she received the Lord Mayor's Award for woodcuts and was elected a Fellow of the Royal Society of Painter-Printmakers.

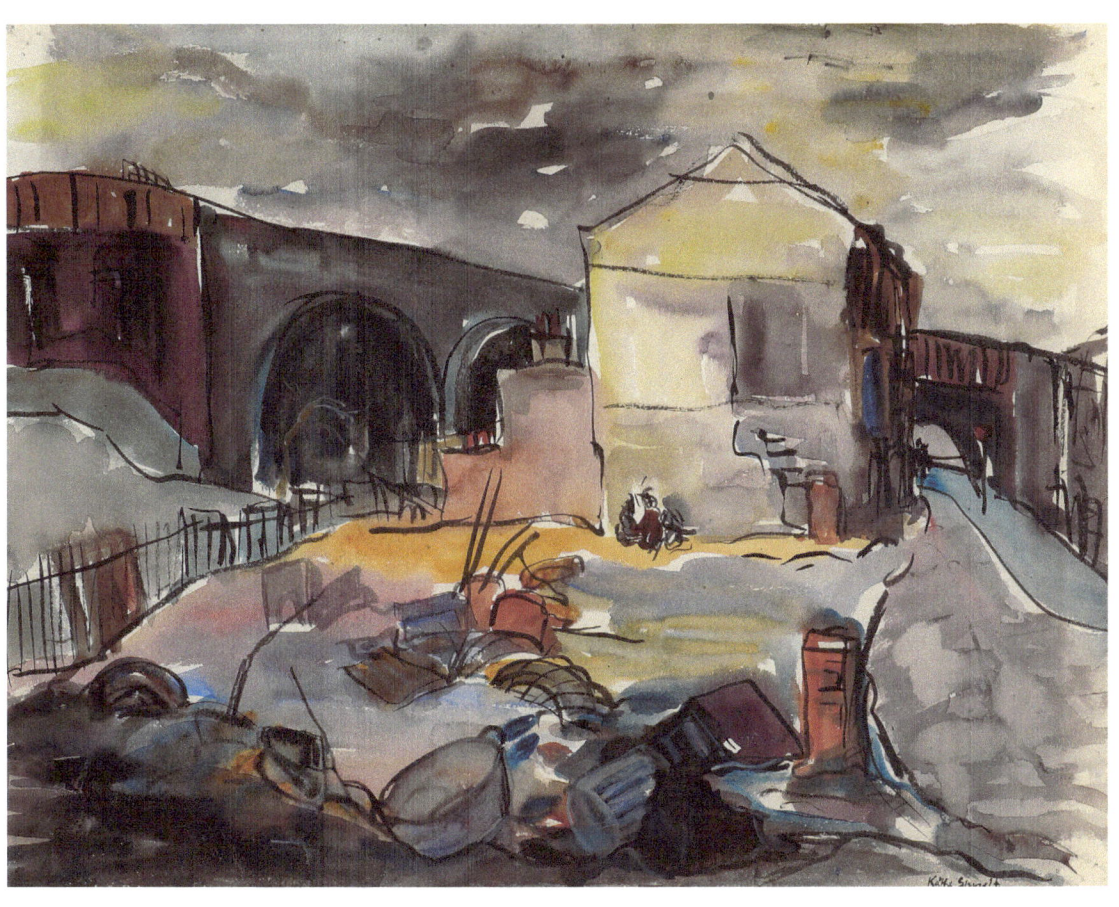

Walter Herz
(1909, Czechoslovakia- 1965, London, England)

Samson, 1947
Oil and gouache on paper
67.5 x 83.5 cm

Ben Uri Collection
Gift from V.V.Rosenfeld

Immigrated to Great Britain 1939

Walter Herz was born in 1909 in Czechoslovakia, then part of the Austro-Hungarian Empire, and practised as a lawyer before immigrating to London in 1939. After the war he retrained, becoming Chief Artist at Heros Publicity studios, a commercial art venture founded with Victor Ross, and a noted book illustrator. He produced leaflets and fundraising material for Zionist organisations and illustrated numerous books on Jewish subjects, among them *Silver Wing, Golden Harp: Jewish Stories for Children*, *The Golden Thread* and *The Everlasting Nay*. He also designed the Holocaust Memorial for the Leicester Synagogue and the official poster for the 1948 London Olympic Games. Herz was also a great collector of books and artefacts and donated his collection to the University of Jerusalem. *Samson* is an impressionistic rendering of the last of the judges of the ancient Israelites' death in the Temple of Dagon.

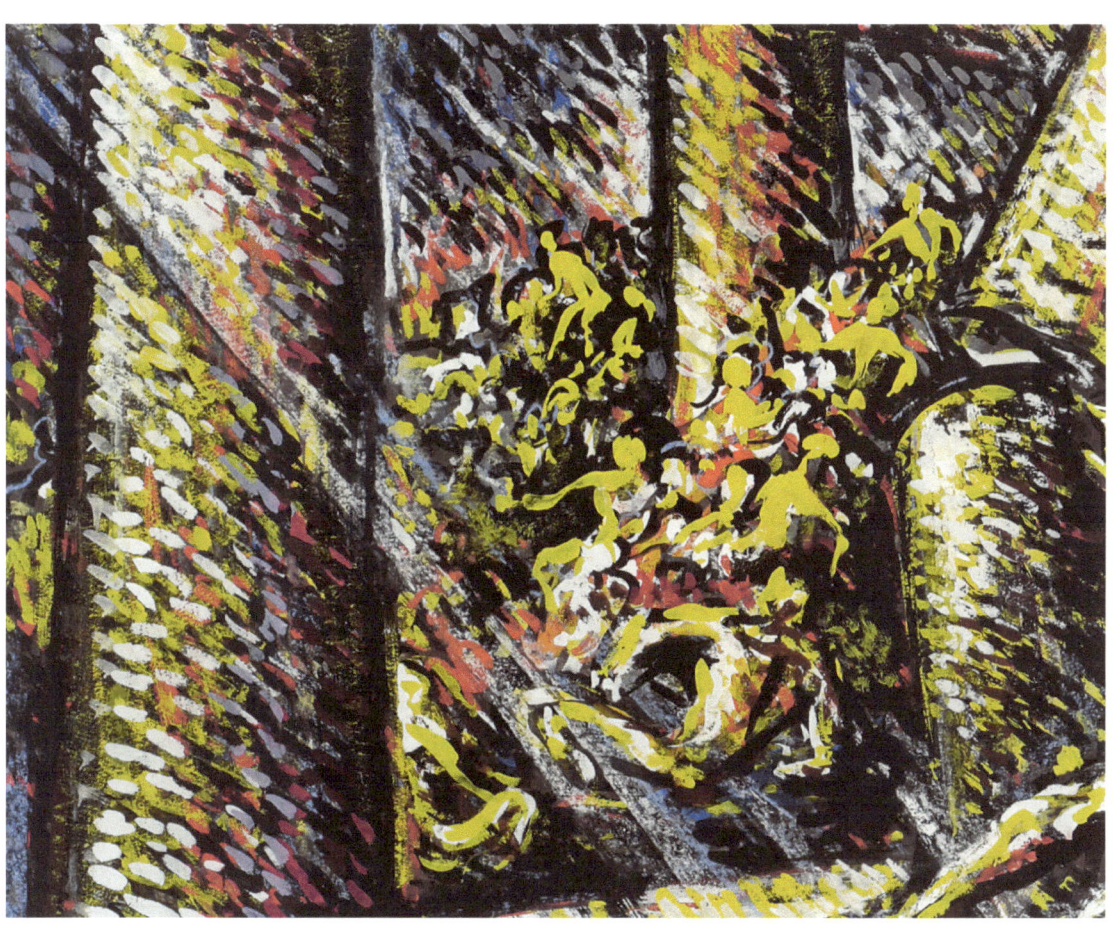

Scarlet Nikolska

(1949, Ostrava, Czechoslovakia)

Sabbath in Prague

Oil on canvas
100.5 x 80.5 cm

Ben Uri Collection
Presented by Dr Arnold Horwell 1995

Immigrated to Great Britain 1974

Scarlet Nikolska was born in Ostrava, Czechoslovakia on 2nd July 1949. She was a pupil of the Czech Expressionist painter Karel Soucek at the Academy of Fine Arts in Prague where she studied from 1969-74. She settled in England in the year of her graduation and had a solo show at Ben Uri in 1975. *The Daily Telegraph* observed that it reflected "the history and the spiritual tradition of her Jewish faith through the figures and forms she lived among in the Jewish ghetto [...] a remarkable record of a way of life and thought which is now dying out". In her early years, Nikolska's paintings, "a blend of scenes encountered in Prague, Cracow and Budapest" indicate a kind of affectionate piety for a vanished world evoked, as in *Sabbath in Prague*, through the use of ochres and browns enlivened, in this case, by blue, white and yellow. She later travelled widely including to the USA and Israel relocating with her family to Brussels and subsequently to Paris.

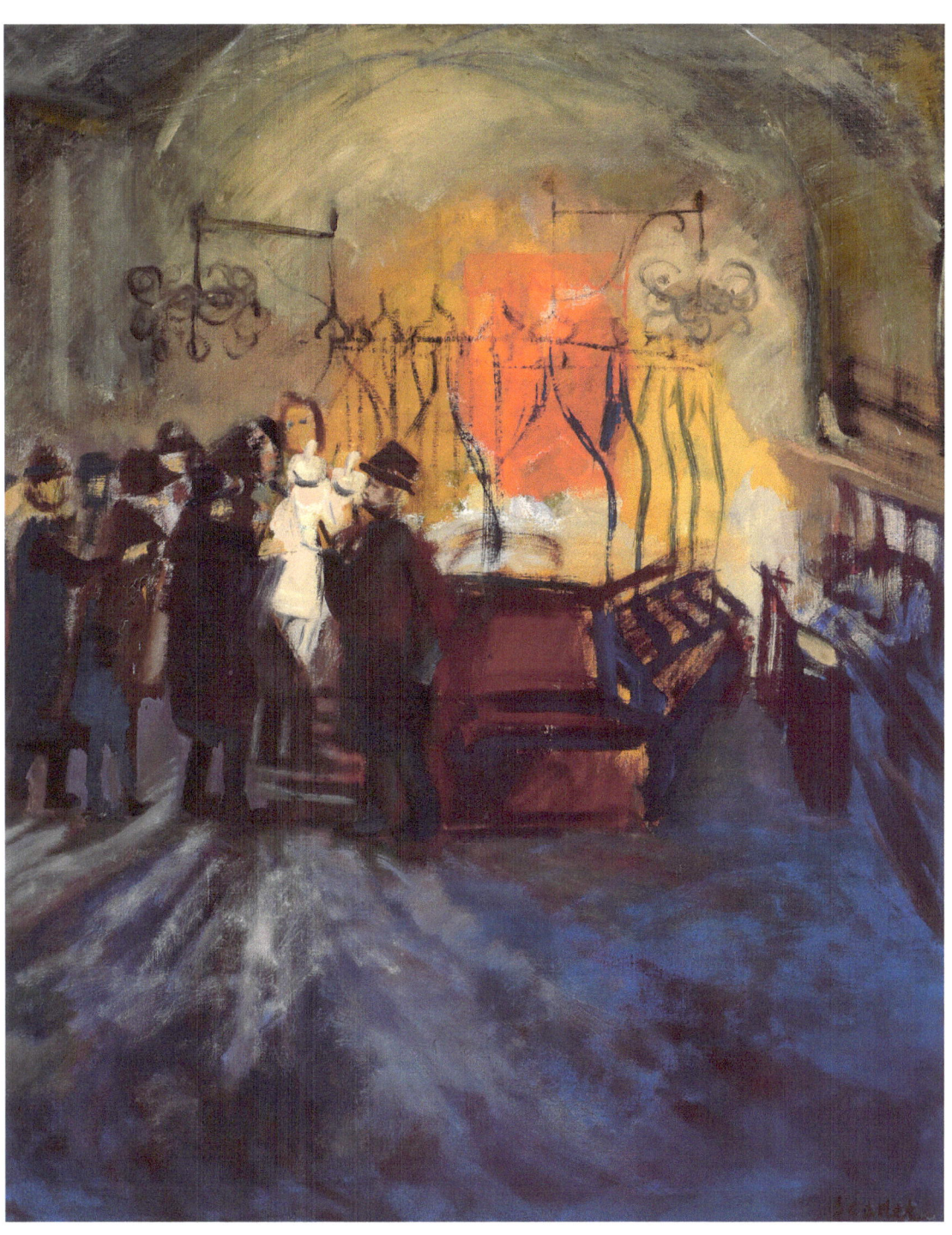

Irena Sedlecká

(1928, Pilsen, Czechoslovakia)

Baudelaire in the guise of Faust with the Phantom of Mephistopheles, 1987

Bronze

72.2 x 36 x 30cm

Signed and dated "SEDLECKA 87" and numbered "1/3" with the Pangolin Edition foundry mark

Studio of Irena Sedlecká

Immigrated to Great Britain 1966

Emotive and striking, *Baudelaire in the guise of Faust with the Phantom of Mephistophele*s is commonly considered to be Sedlecká's masterwork, cementing her reputation as the most distinguished Czechoslovak-born figurative sculptor working in Britain today. Cast in bronze shortly after 2000, a resin bronze cast was exhibited in London at the Society of Portrait Sculptors in *FACE 2005* (57).

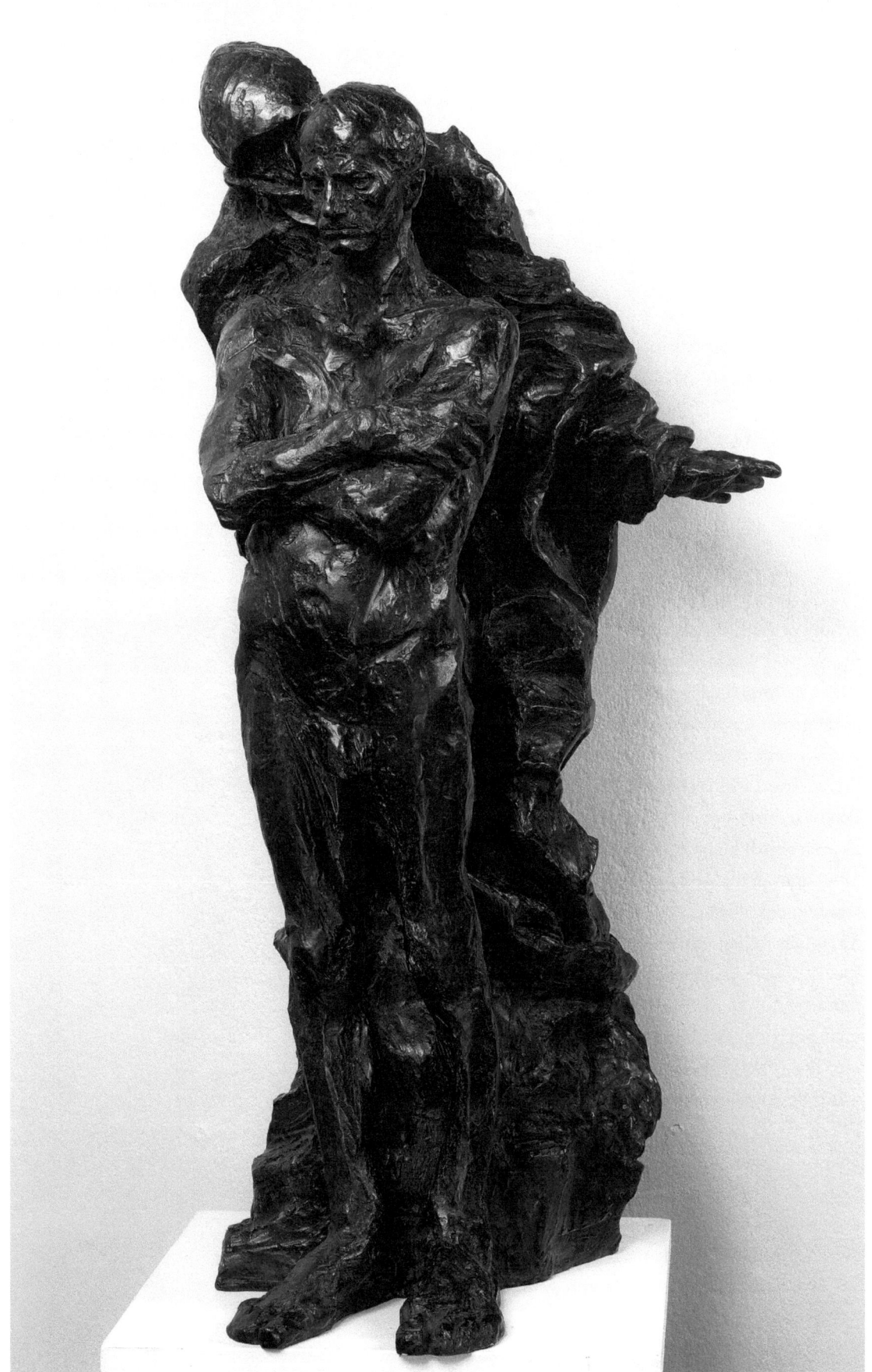

Shraga Weil

(1918, Nitra Czechoslovakia-2009, Israel)

Symbols of Passover (The Ram)

Lithograph on paper
46.5 x 61cm

Ben Uri Collection
Presented by Mrs. Alice Schwab

Immigrated to Israel 1948

Born into a traditional Jewish family in Nitra, Czechoslovakia in 1918, and later apprenticed to a local sculptor, Weil studied at the National School of Arts, Prague. Upon the outbreak of the Second World War, Weil fled to Budapest, where he forged papers for the Hungarian underground. Arrested in 1943, he was sent with his wife to a concentration camp, then prison, from which they escaped in 1944. Post-war, he designed books for the Jewish Zionist youth Hehalutz movement, and in 1948 immigrated to Israel. He studied at the Académie des Beaux Arts in Paris (1952-53) under Italian Futurist Gino Severini, specialising in printmaking, reliefs and wall murals. From the 1960s onwards, he began incorporating Jewish symbols and iconography into his works. The sacrificial or Paschal lamb was traditionally slaughtered on the eve of Passover and eaten on the first night of the Jewish Passover holiday with bitter herbs and matzo. Weil is best-known for his architectural door designs for the Knesset building's main entrance and the President's residence, and the Tel Aviv Great Synagogue's ceramic walls.

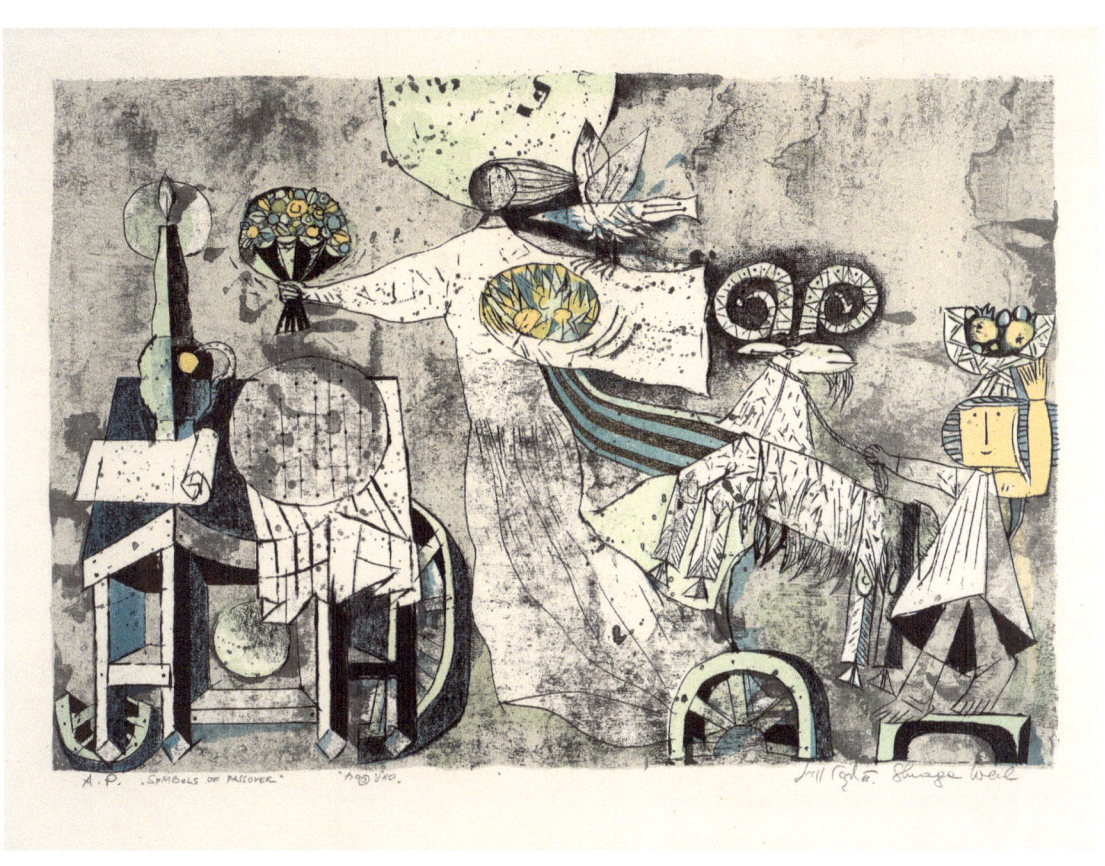

A.P.   „SYMBOLS OF PASSOVER"   חג הפסח.   still right. Savage Weil

Jacob Bornfriend (Jakub Bauernfreund)

(1904, Zborov, Czechoslovakia – 1976, London, England)

Blue Grey Fishes, 1960

Oil on canvas
61.6 x 49 cm

Ben Uri Collection
Gift from Alexander Margulies 1987

Immigrated to Great Britain 1939

Born in Zborov, Czechoslovakia in 1904, Bornfriend trained at the Academy of Fine Arts, Prague under Willi Nowak, developing an expressionistic style. After the Nazi occupation, he fled to Britain in 1939, losing much of his work in the process. In London he became part of a group of artists known as the Continental British School of Painting which also included Oskar Kokoschka. His work was exhibited at German émigré Jack Bilbo's Modern Art Gallery (1941-48), the Czechoslovak Institute (1945), by dealers Roland, Browse & Delbanco in the 1950s and 60s, and the Ben Uri Gallery (1974). In 1957 he was commissioned by architect Eugene Rosenberg to design a mural for Jews' College, London (now the London School of Jewish Studies). From the late 1950s Bornfriend experimented with abstraction in dialogue with British Abstractionists Patrick Heron and Peter Lanyon, using rhythmic patterns to convey a certain buoyancy of spirit and to capture the "the dynamism of abundance" which he perceived in the British landscape.

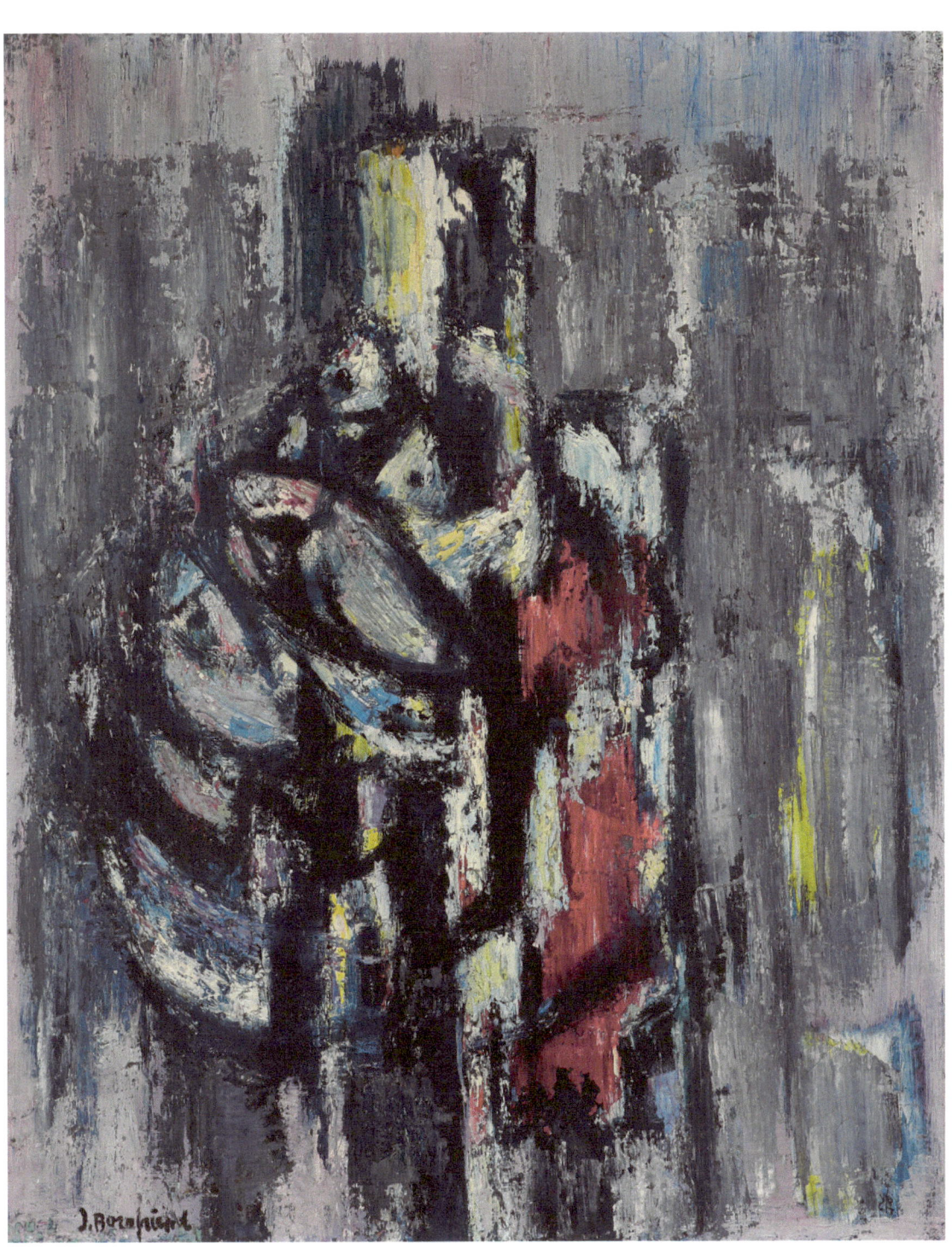

Yehuda Bacon

(1929, Moravská Ostrava, Czechoslovakia)

Variations on a Theme (10 Coloured Etchings), 1957

Coloured etchings on paper
24.6 x 10.1 cm

Ben Uri Collection
Presented by Dr Israel Feldman 1957

Immigrated to Palestine 1946

Yehuda Bacon was born into an Orthodox
Jewish family in Moravská Ostrava,
Czechoslovakia in 1929. In 1942, aged
thirteen, he was deported with his family to
Terezin (Theresienstadt) Ghetto, where he
met and studied under artist inmates Leo
Haas, Karel Fleischmann, Peter Kien and Otto
Unger, then to Auschwitz in 1943. He was
liberated from Mauthausen on 5th May 1945.
After the war he returned to Czechoslovakia,
before settling in Palestine, where he studied
at the Bezalel School of Arts and Design.
Following a year in London at the Central
School of Arts and Crafts, he travelled and
studied in Italy and the United States. His
teaching career began in Jerusalem in 1951,
and in 1959, he returned to the Bezalel School
as a member of staff. While the majority
of Bacon's work deals with the horrors he
witnessed during the Holocaust – feeling he
has a responsibility to tell his story – *Variations
on a Theme* possesses an air of uncharacteristic
optimism and is a celebration of form
and colour.

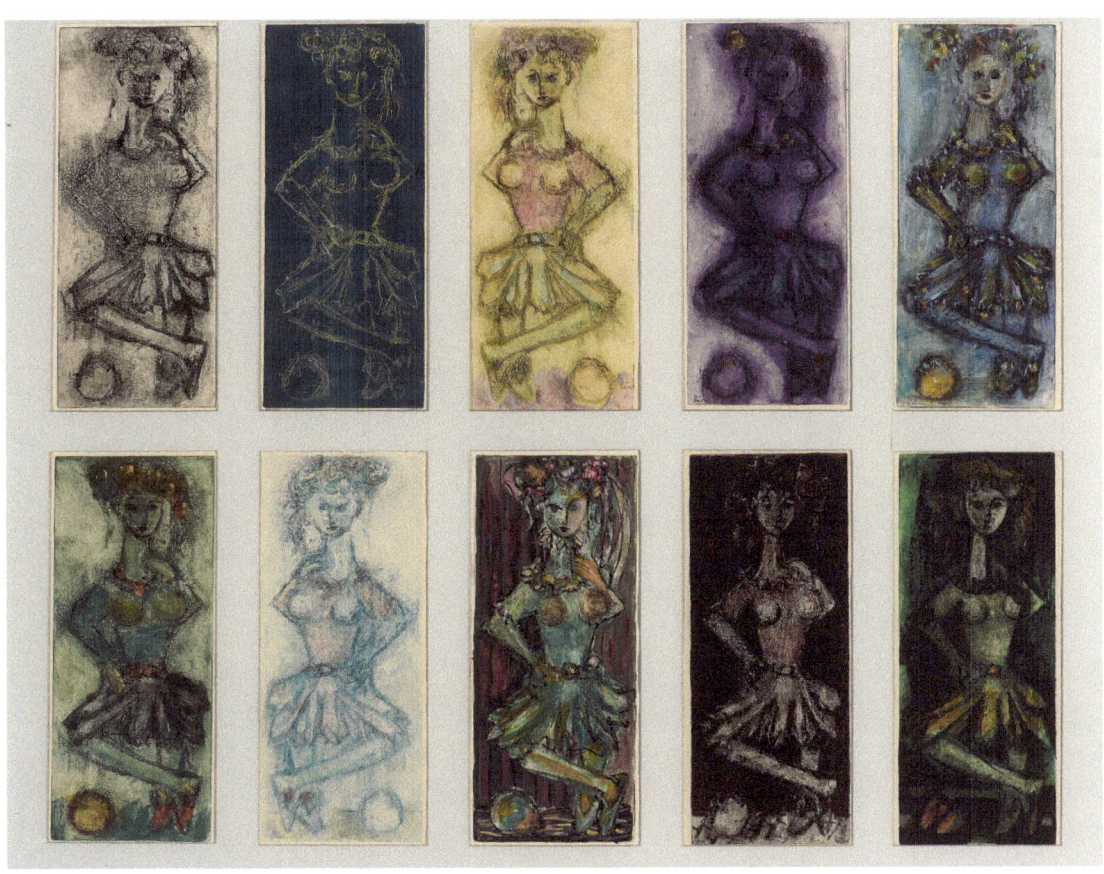

Franta Bělský

(1921, Brno, Czechoslovakia-2000, Sutton Courtenay, Oxfordshire, England)

Joy-Ride, 1958

Bronze
62 x 36 x 31cm
Signed "F Bělský" in the wax on the integral circular base

The Estate of Franta Belsky

Immigrated to Great Britain 1939

Sculptor Franta Bělský was born in Brno, Czechoslovakia, the son of eminent economist Joseph Bělský, in 1921. His studies at the Academy of Fine Arts in Prague having been interrupted by the Nazi invasion of Czechoslovakia, Bělský, along with his family was forced to flee, seeking refuge in Britain. He returned to Prague after the war to find that 22 of his relations had perished in the Holocaust. He fled to England for a second time to escape from the Communist takeover of 1948. Subsequent commissions in Britain included numerous architectural sculptures for schools in Hertfordshire and Essex, *Triga* (1958), a 30ft high group of three rearing horses created for Caltex House, Knightsbridge, London, *Joy-Ride* for Stevenage New Town Centre (1958) and a monumental fountain, conceived as a 'sculptural counterpart' to Bach's Toccata and Fugue in D, for the Shell Building, South Bank, London (1959-61). He was also responsible for the 9 foot statue of Lord Mountbatten which stands in London's Horse Guards Parade, unveiled in 1983. Hidden in the left leg of the statue is a jam jar containing coins, press cuttings and details of the sculptor's commission. Bělský was a regular exhibitor at the Royal Academy from 1943 and is the only sculptor to have modelled four generations of the British Royal family. He was a member of the Council of the Royal Society of British Sculptors, a governor of St Martin's School of Art and a founder member of the Society of Portrait Sculptors, later its President. Following his first wife's death Bělský married the sculptor Irena Sedlecká, numerous examples of whose work can also be seen in Britain. This sculpture, a young mother and boy composition, is a cast taken from a competition model for the 1½ life-size sculpture commissioned by Stevenage Development Corporation,1958, for the Town Square, Stevenage. Made, in the artist's own words, "for a set of very good reasons, half of them formal, half, one might say, sentimental", he felt it important that the sculpture, in situ, be "comfortably within reach of hands, the base low enough for children to climb on and if the surfaces were inviting and pleasing to touch – an object of affection and not a forbidding idol forcing a respectful distance".

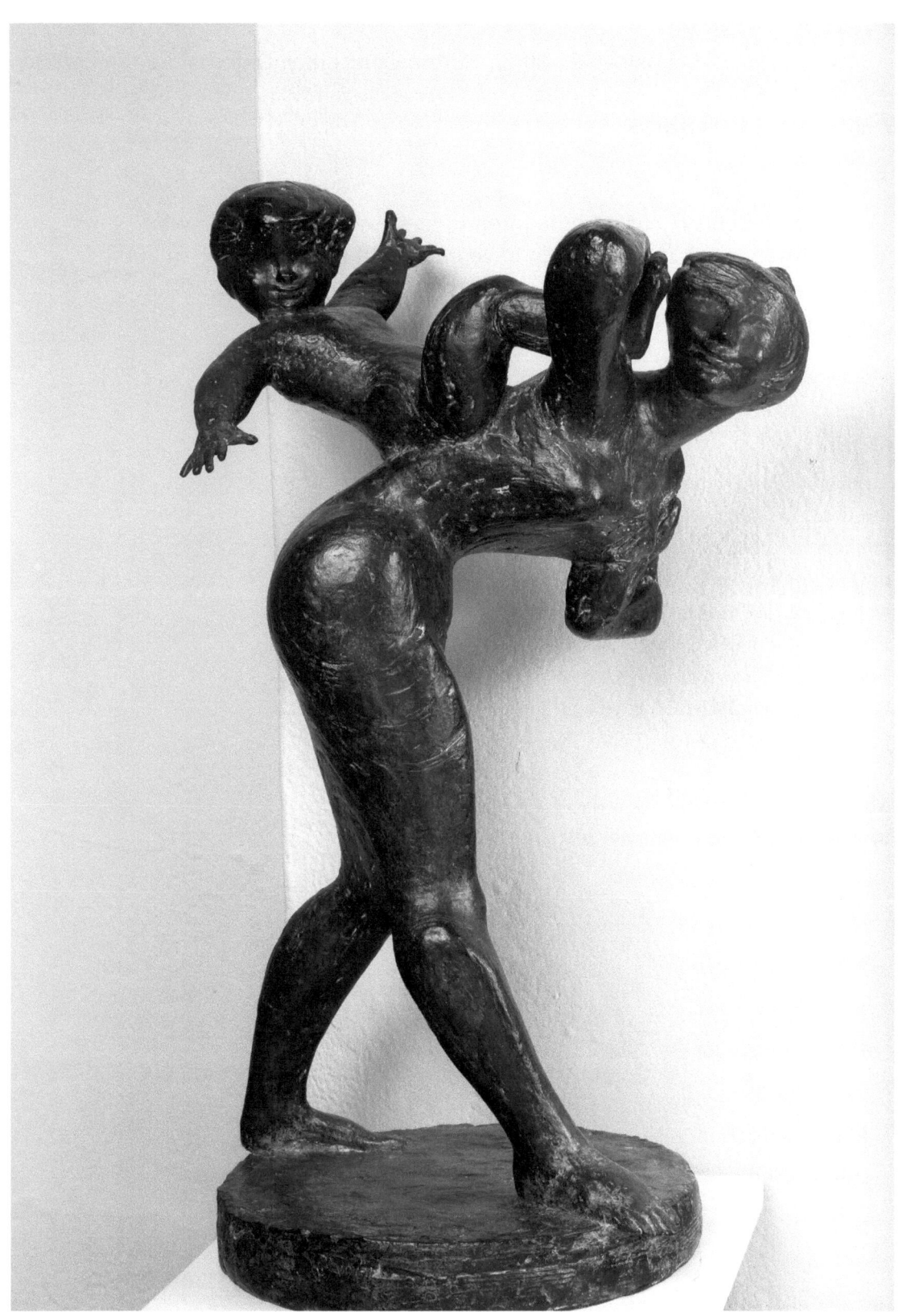

Franta Bělský

(1921, Brno, Czechoslovakia-2000, Sutton Courtenay, Oxfordshire, England)

Pepina, late 1990s

Bronze
44 x 32 x 24cm
Signed "F Belsky" cut into the integral base, and "4/6" in the wax
No foundry mark but known to have been cast at Burlingfield in 2003

Private Collection

Immigrated to Great Britain 1939

The model for this fountain figure is not
illustrated in *Franta Bělský – Sculpture*
published in 1992, thus it can be dated to
the late 1990s as confirmed by the sculptor's
widow, Irena Sedlecká. A bronze cast of
Pepina was exhibited in the Salon, 1998, and a
subsequent bronze cast was given to the John
Radcliffe Hospital, Oxford, in recognition
of the care received there by Bělský. The
earlier soft blue-green patina proved not to be
weather resistant and this cast was re-patinated
by Pangolin Editions Foundry in 2018.

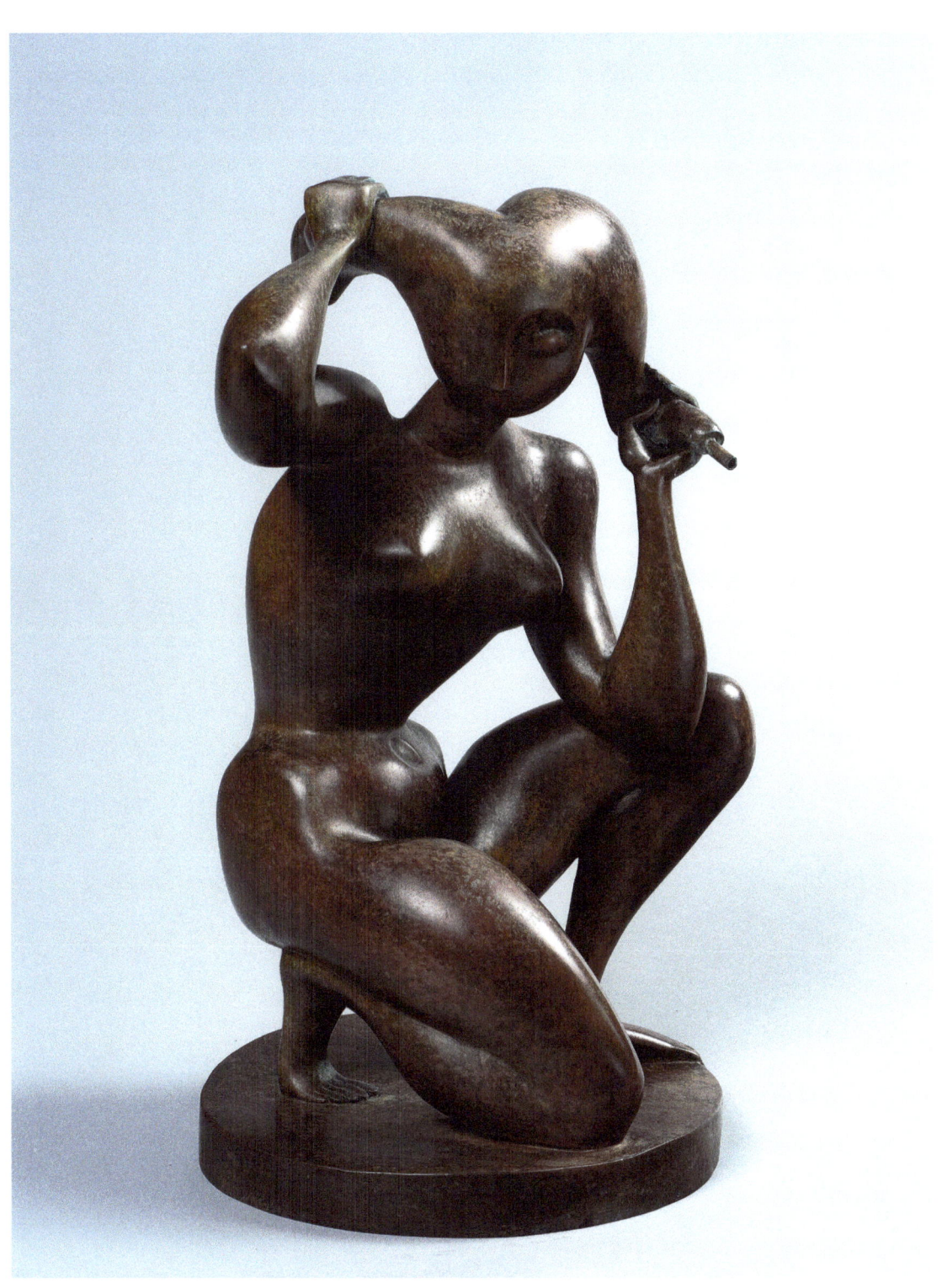

Franta Bělský

(1921, Brno, Czechoslovakia-2000, Sutton Courtenay, Oxfordshire, England)

Venusform III, 1969

Bronze
26.5 x 13 x 10cm
Signed "F Belsky" in the wax on lower left buttock
No foundry mark

Private Collection

Immigrated to Great Britain 1939

This sculpture is a maquette for a much larger version measuring more than a metre in height and made in 1969. The full-scale version of this composition, in aluminium resin (Estate of Franta Bělský) is illustrated in *Franta Bělský – Sculpture* published by Richter, Prague and A. Zwemmer Ltd., 1992.

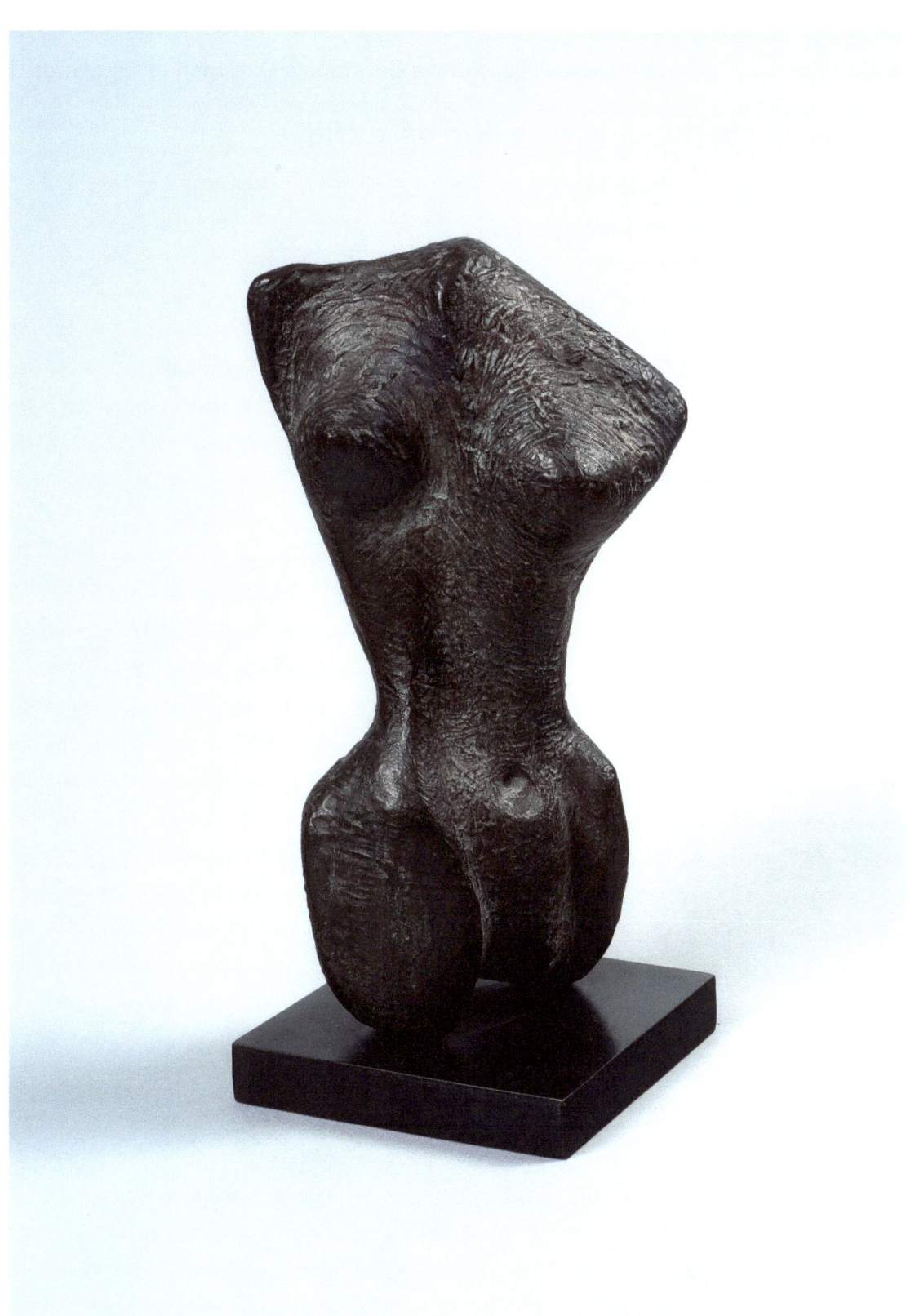

Franta Bělský

(1921, Brno, Czechoslovakia-2000, Sutton Courtenay, Oxfordshire, England)

Woman Crouching with a Mirror, c.1960s

Bronze
19.9 x 26 x 18cm
Unsigned studio cast with no marks

Private Collection

Immigrated to Great Britain 1939

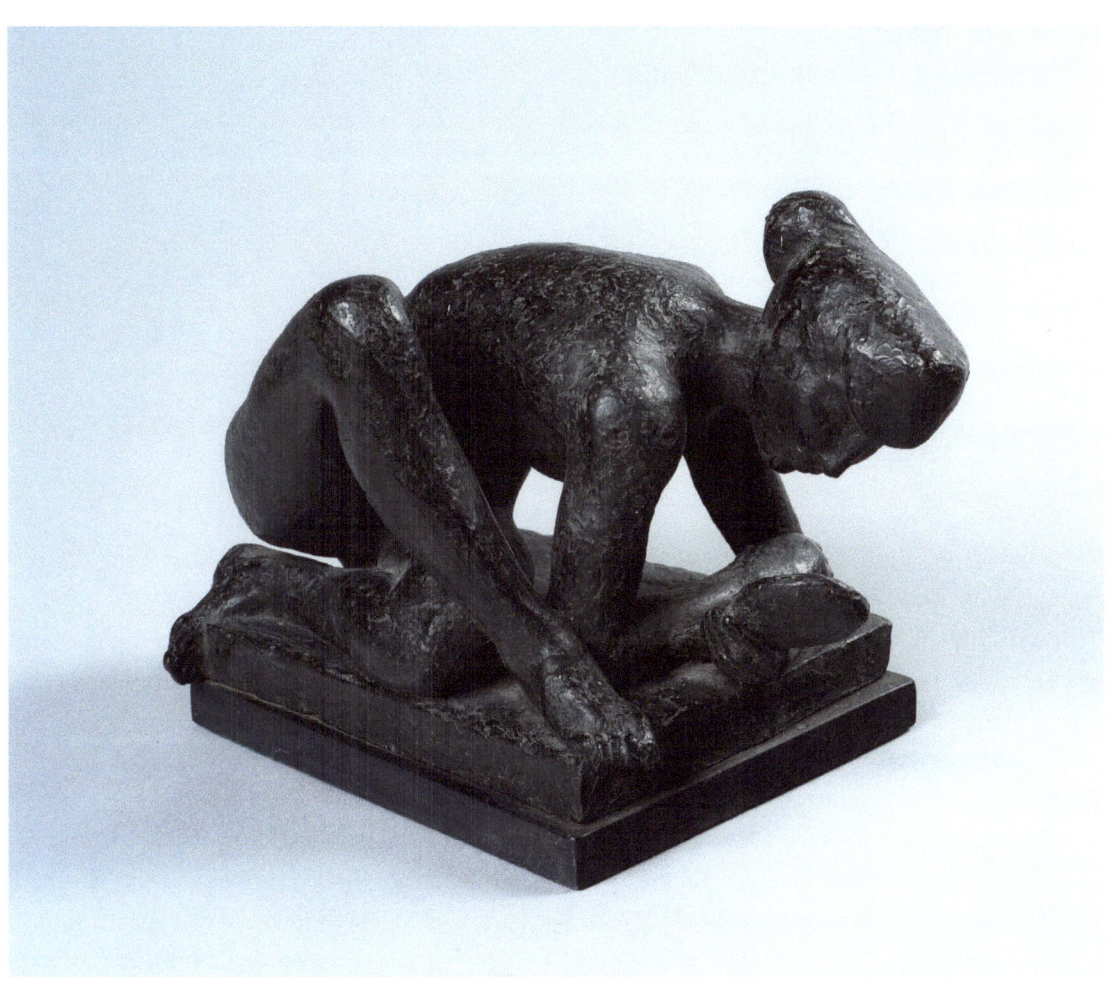

Anita Mandl

(1926, Prague, Czechoslovakia)

Owl 1, 1969

Rio Rosewood
28.5 x 17.3 wide, 13.5cm
No signature or marks

Private Collection

Immigrated to Great Britain 1939

Anita Mandl was born in Prague and came to England in 1939, as one of the so-called 'Winton children', who travelled on a Quaker-sponsored Kindertransport organised by British humanitarian Nicholas Winton. She lost both of her parents in the Holocaust. On leaving Dudley High School she trained as a zoologist at Birkbeck College, University of London, gaining a first class honours degree in 1947. She joined the staff at the Medical School, University of Birmingham and was awarded a PhD in 1951 followed by a DSc in 1960. During this period she attended evening classes in sculpture at the Birmingham College of Art. In 1965, she married and moved to Devon where she set up a sculpture studio in her garden and has been carving ever since.

In 1978 she was made a member of the Royal West of England Academy and in 1980 she became a Fellow of the Royal Society of British Sculptors. The majority of Mandl's sculptures are simplified animal forms with highly polished surfaces in which extraneous details are eliminated in order to enhance the beauty of the natural materials with which she works. While Mandl's early carvings were mostly in hardwoods she has subsequently turned to alabaster, soapstone and marble and for some time experimented with two-tone effects and polished areas with chiselled or scratched finishes or inlaid resins. Unusually for a stone carver, many of Mandl's pieces are also cast in bronze. *Owl I* has been exhibited widely since its completion on 26th November 1969.

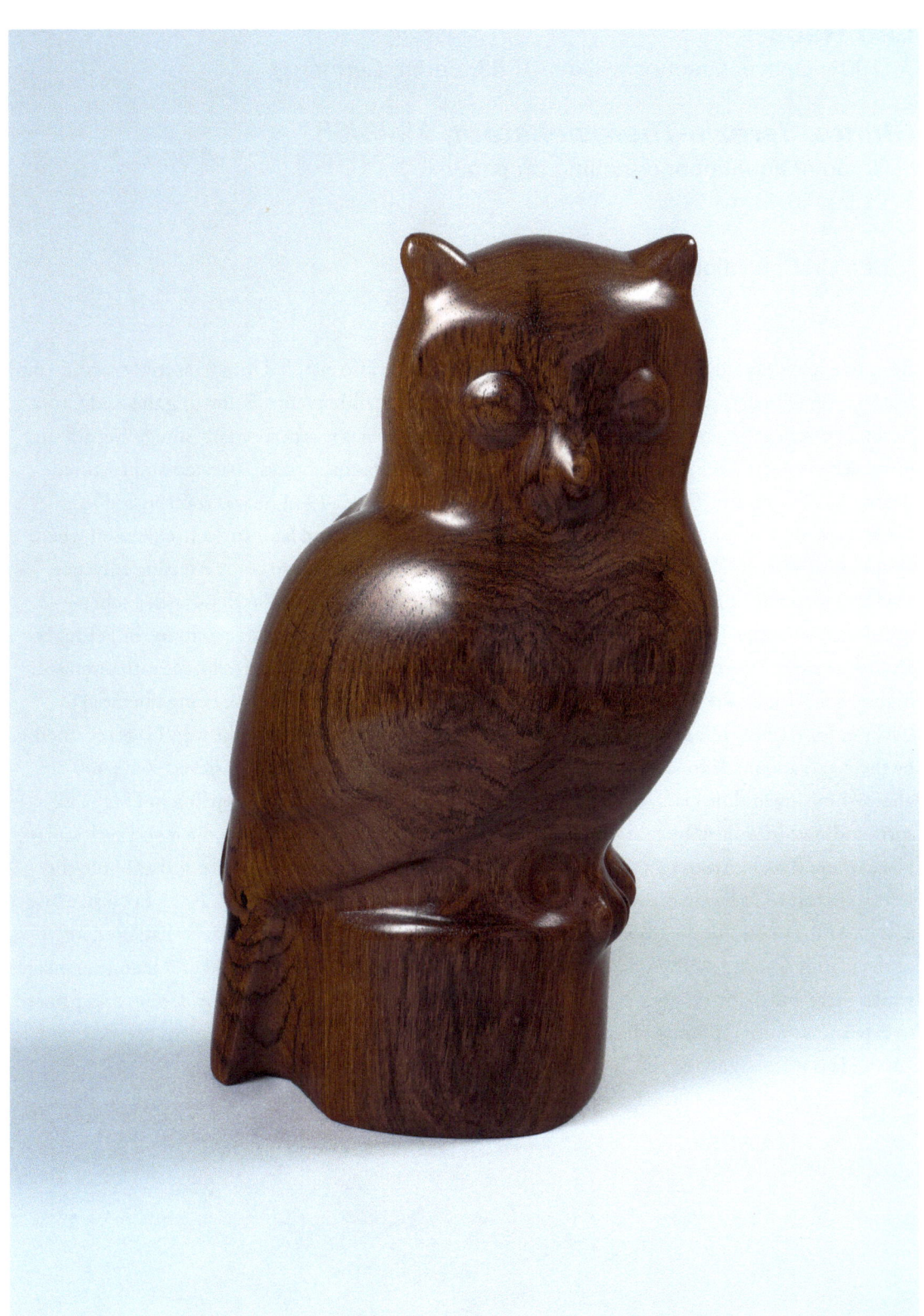

Leo Haas

(1901, Opava, Czechoslovakia –1983, Berlin, Germany)

Ghetto, Terezín-Theresienstadt, 1945/66

Drypoint aquatint and etching on paper
21.5 x 28.4 cm

Ben Uri Collection

Born to a Jewish family in Opava, Moravia, in 1901, Leo Haas studied in Karlsruhe and Berlin between 1919 and 1922, where he was influenced by German Expressionism and the works of Goya and Toulouse-Lautrec. He was arrested in 1939 for helping German communists to cross the border illegally and sent into forced labour. In September 1942 he was deported to the Terezin (Theresienstadt) ghetto, north of Prague. In advance of a high profile visit by the International Red Cross in June 1944, Terezin was redesigned by the Nazis and made to look like a 'model ghetto' housing middle-class Jews in pleasant surroundings. In reality, Terezin was a brutal place where Czech, Austrian and German Jews were forced to live in overcrowded and unsanitary conditions. About a quarter of the mainly Czech Jewish inmates died whilst there and many others were deported to extermination camps in the East. As an artist, Haas was assigned to the Technical Department to illustrate propaganda material,

which also enabled him to secretly record real and terrible events. Following the Red Cross visit, Haas was accused of "smuggling atrocity propaganda abroad", arrested and tortured. In October 1944 he was transported to Auschwitz and later to Sachsenhausen where he was assigned to counterfeiting currency as part of 'Operation Bernhard', a scheme to destabilize the British economy. In February 1945 he was transported to Mauthausen and then to Ebensee, before being liberated by the Americans. After the war, Haas returned to Terezín, where he retrieved some 400 of his hidden artworks. Settling in Prague he worked as a newspaper editor and caricaturist, was reunited with his wife and adopted the son of his friend Bedrich Fritta (also an artist imprisoned in Terezin), who had died in Auschwitz. This powerful and haunting image is one of ten in the Ben Uri Collection printed after the war using the original plate created during the Holocaust.

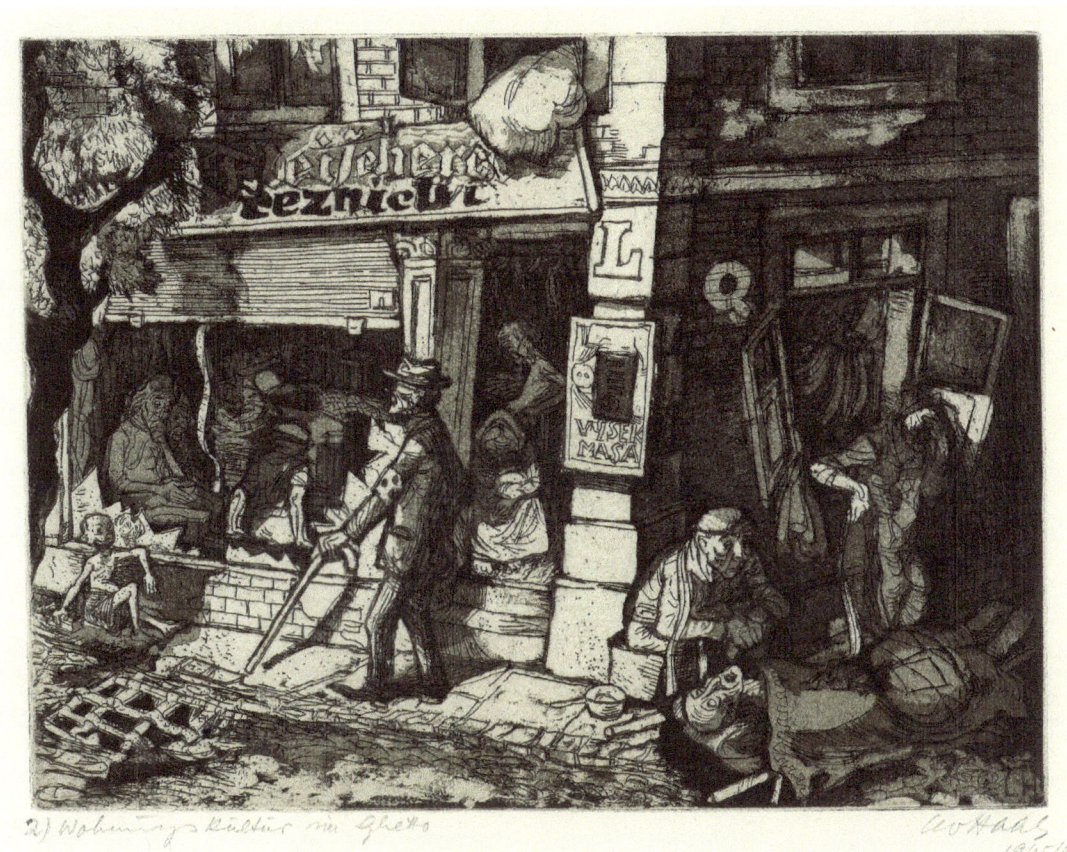

2) Wohnungs-Kultur im Ghetto

A. v. Haas
1945/66

Leo Haas

(1901, Opava, Czechoslovakia –1983, Berlin, Germany)

Life, The Market Place, Terezín-Theresienstadt, 1945/66

Drypoint and aquatint on paper
26.7 x 34 cm

Ben Uri Collection

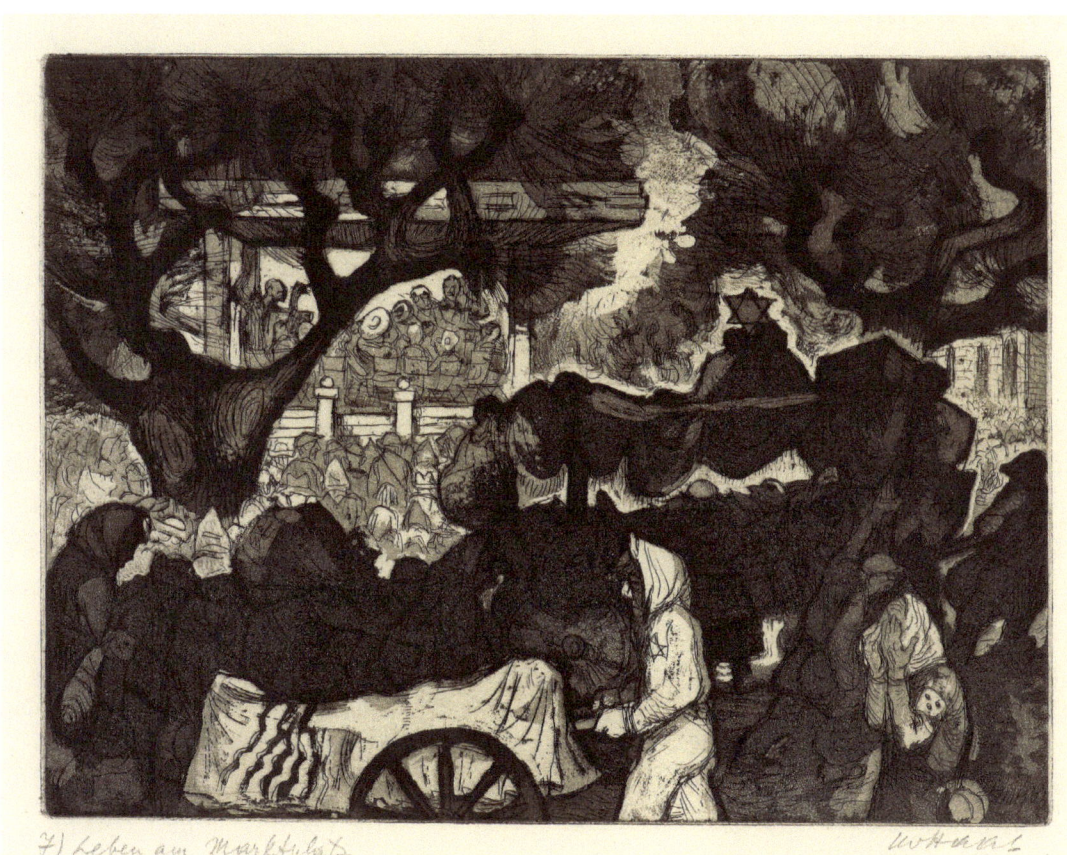

7) Leben am Marktplatz

W.Hacks
1945/66

Geza Szobel

(1905, Komárno, Slovakia – 1963, Boulogne-Billancourt, France)

Outside the Prison, 1942

Pen and ink on vellum
17 x 25cm
Private Collection

Immigrated to Great Britain early 1940s

Geza Szobel was born in Komárno, then part of the Austro-Hungarian Empire and studied at the Fine Arts Academy of Prague before moving to Paris in 1927, where he became the student of Fernand Léger. The modern French art movements influenced his works significantly but a brief stay in Berlin also introduced him to German Expressionism, which made Szobel decide to return to Prague. Eventually, he returned to Paris where he would settle, and became friends with avant-garde artists Chagall, Le Corbusier, Aragon, Lucien Hervé and Sonia and Robert Delaunay. In this inspiring and vibrant atmosphere, Szóbel's painting fused fauvism, expressionism, surrealism and cubism. He joined the Czechoslovak Army in France during the Second World War, finally succeeding in reaching England in the early 1940s after many painful experiences. From his personal recollections and from the stories of his fellow soldiers who reached France from Nazi occupied countries, a series of drawings was born. Szobel's work was discovered by art critic Herbert Read and his drawings, grouped under the title *Civilisation* (including *Outside the Prison*), were exhibited at the Czechoslovak Institute in London in 1942, followed by the V&A, alongside Goya's *Los Desastres de la Guerra* and Jacques Callot's *Les Misères et Malheurs de la Guerre*. They were published by Penguin Books the same year. Szobel's drawings, in the creation of which "he … used a sprayed technique of shading, done with a brush through a net screen, … give his sketches of murder and torture an effective air as of horrors too fearful to be dragged into the full light of day".

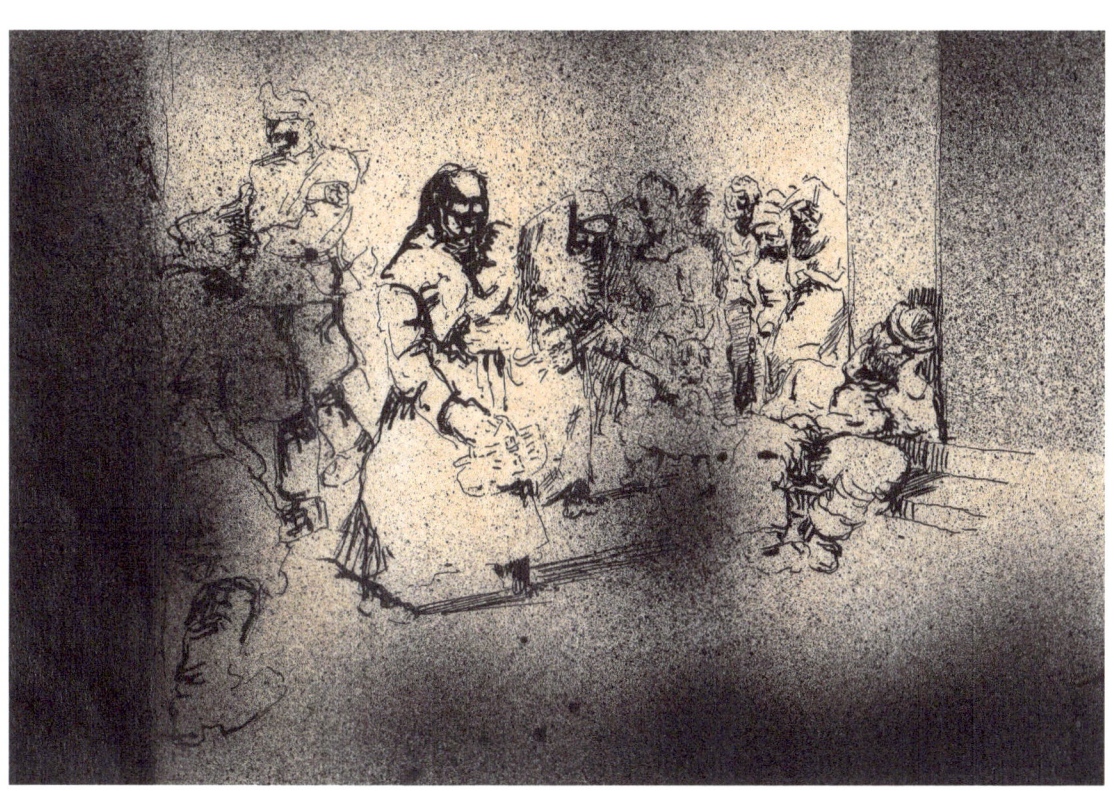

Irena Sedlecká
(1928, Pilsen, Czechoslovakia)

Franz Kafka, 1967
Bronze
55.6 x 12.5 wide x 11.3cm
Signed "SEDLECKA" cut into the wax and "1/3 +
foundry mark "PE" for Pangolin Edition

Private Collection

Immigrated to Great Britain 1966

Irena Sedlecká born on September 7, 1928 in Plzeň, Czechoslovakia, is a sculptor and Fellow of the Royal British Society of Sculptors. After training at the Academy of Fine Arts in Prague under Karel Pokorný, she was awarded the Lenin Prize for sculpture before fleeing the communist regime in 1966. She travelled first to Yugoslavia with her family on the pretence of a camping holiday, across the border into Italy, then to France and finally to Britain. She had hoped to return to Czechoslovakia in 1968 but was deterred by the USSR's brutal repression of the 'Prague Spring' uprising. Her third husband Franta Bělský, already living in England, helped her to secure exhibiting opportunities. Both became deeply involved with the Society of Portrait Sculptors and played key roles in its revitalisation (1984-96) after a period of virtual hibernation. Reflecting on her life in Prague prior to immigration, in an interview some ten years ago, Sedlecká mused: "Reading *The Trial*, I understood for the first time what it means to be Czech. He made sense of those terrible times when the authorities would simply pull you in for questioning, without your ever knowing the reason. That experience has shaped our national psyche". It was Sedlecká's dream to create a series of Kafka-inspired bronzes as a tribute to the author who gave her a sense of identity. It is interesting to note too the work's resonance with Alberto Giacometti's severely attenuated figures and that it was created the year after the Swiss sculptor's death. The plaster model for this sculpture was exhibited at the Society of Portrait Sculptors, London, 1967 and cast in bronze shortly after 2000.

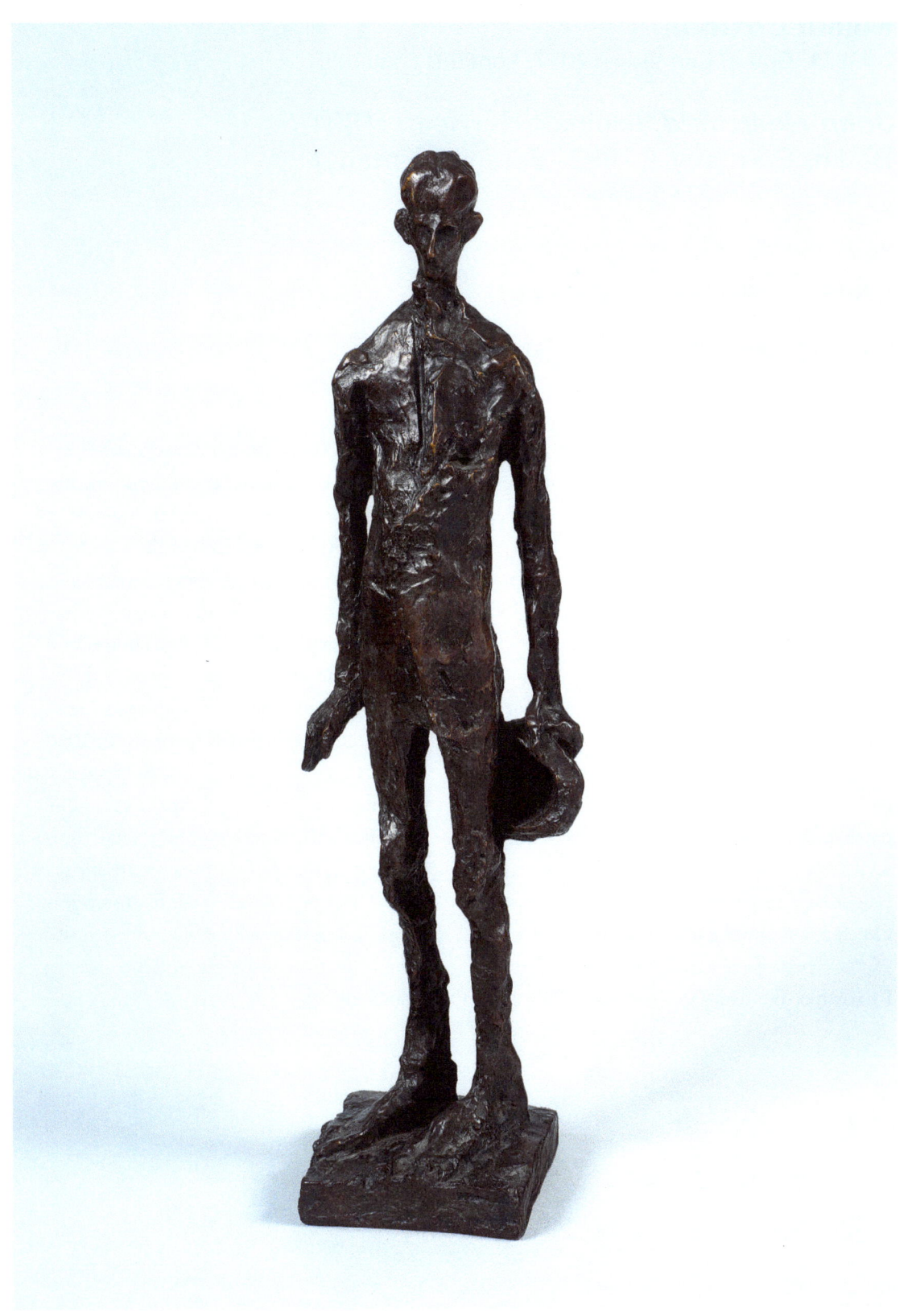

Milein Cosman
(1921, Gotha, Germany – 2017, London, England)

John Heartfield, (Helmut Herzfeld) (1891, Berlin, Germany – 1968, Berlin, Germany)
Drypoint etching on paper
40 x 30cm

Caroline Uhlman

Immigrated to Great Britain 1939

John Heartfield is best known for his agitprop photomontages and his role in the development of the Dada movement in Berlin. Having anglicised his name in 1916 in response to rampant German nationalism and resultant anti-British sentiment, in 1933 Heartfield fled to Prague, escaping shortly before a raid on his apartment by the Nazi authorities. There he continued his work for the *Arbeiter – Illustrierte-Zeitung,* a widely circulated left-wing weekly edited in Prague between 1933 and 1938 and contributed twice to the international exhibitions of the S.V.U. Mánes, an artists' association founded in Prague that encouraged interaction between Czech artists and the foreign avant-garde. In 1937-38 he became a member of the Oskar-Kokoschka-Bund and in December 1938, with the Nazi invasion of Czechoslovakia imminent, escaped to London with the help of the British Committee for Refugees from Czechoslovakia (later named the Czech Refugee Trust Fund). He stayed for a week or so with the writer Yvonne Kapp, before moving in with fellow German émigré Fred Uhlman and his wife Diana (née Croft) at 47 Downshire Hill in Hampstead. He subsequently returned to Germany in 1950. Milein Cosman fled Germany in 1939, moving to Hampstead in 1946 where she met John Heartfield. She is perhaps best known for her drawings of many of the greatest artistic names of 20th century, as well as for her forty-year-long collaboration with her Viennese husband, the musician, musicologist and broadcaster, Hans Keller.

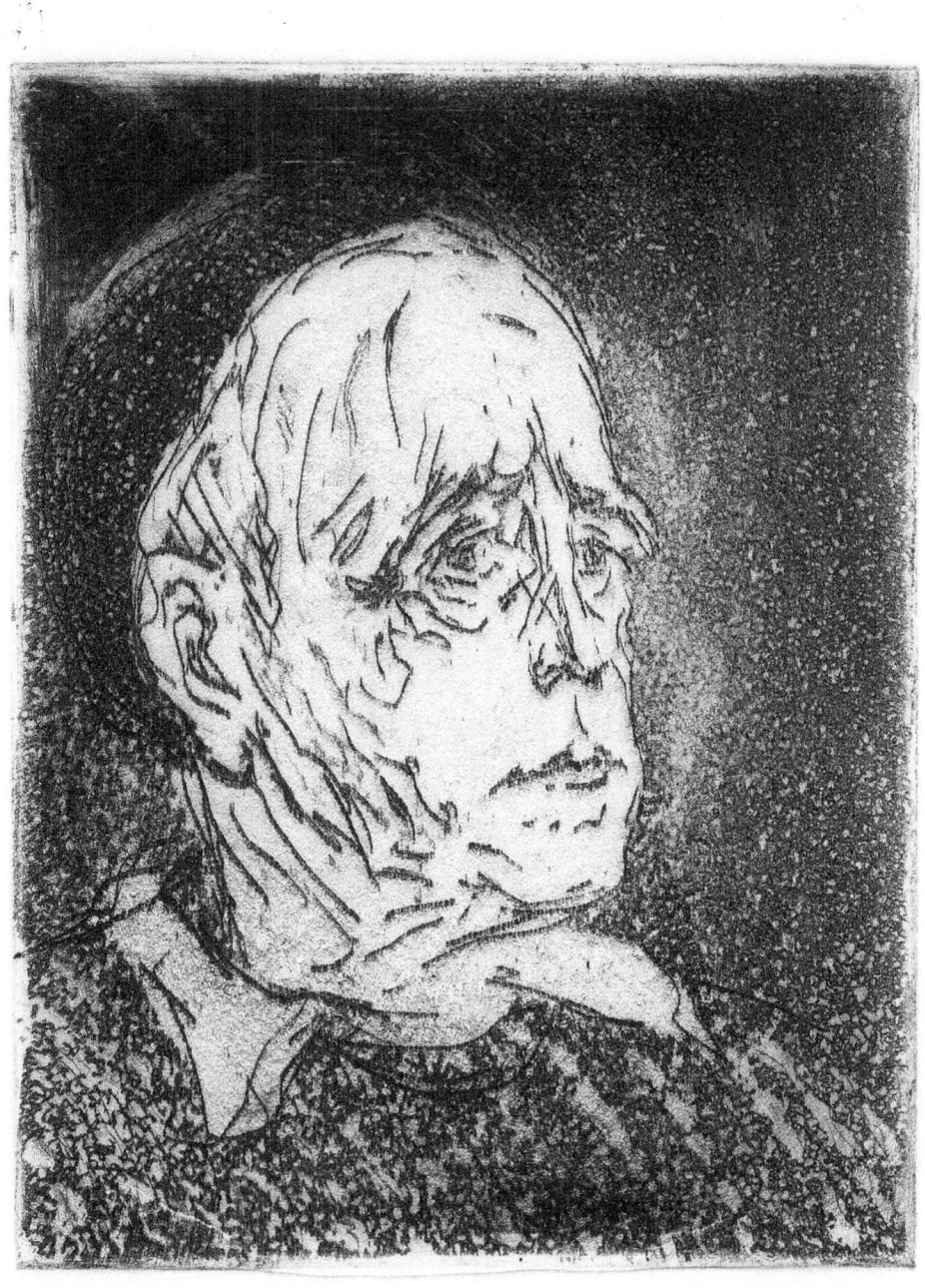

Franta Bělský

(1921, Brno, Czechoslovakia-2000, Sutton Courtenay, Oxfordshire, England)

Wenceslas Hollar, 1983

Bronze

31.1 x 25cm

No inscriptions or foundry mark, but known to have been cast in Prague after 2000.

Private Collection

Immigrated to Great Britain 1939

Bohemian Wenceslas Hollar (1607-1677) was a master etcher and one of the most accomplished and prolific artists of the 17th century. He settled in England in 1637, but moved to Antwerp in about 1644, returning to London in 1652. He illustrated a number of books and produced the celebrated *Views of London* after the Great Fire of 1666. The Czechoslovak Institute, established at President Beneš's behest and formally opened by Anthony Eden, Secretary of State for Foreign Affairs, in January 1941, hosted an exhibition of drawings and engraving by Hollar attended on St George's Day, April 1942 by the Queen Mother. The prime version of this bronze relief, in nickel bronze, forms part of the epitaph in Southwark Cathedral, commissioned in 1983.

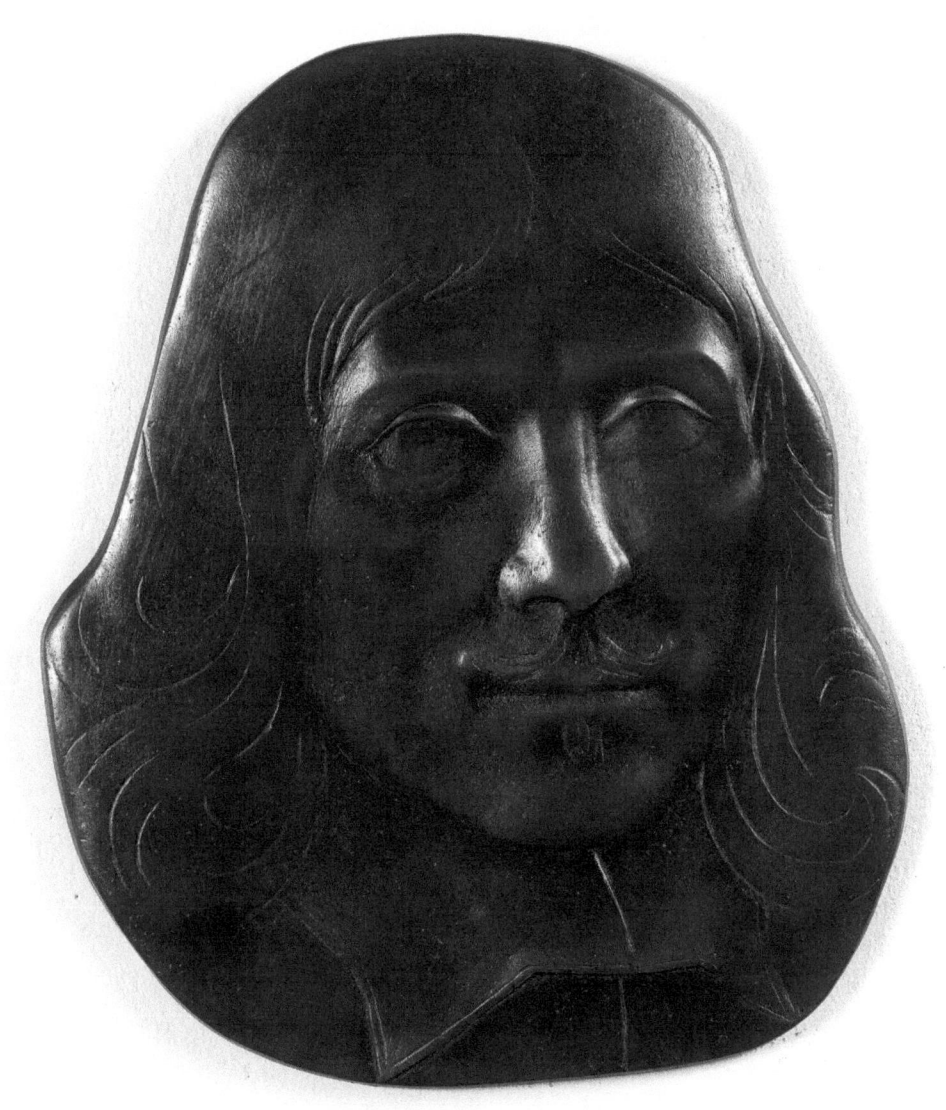

Franta Bělský

(1921, Brno, Czechoslovakia – 2000, Sutton Courtenay, Oxfordshire, England)

Zátopek Military Race Medal, 1948

Struck bronze uniface
8cm diameter
Signed and dated "F. Bělský.48"

Private Collection

Immigrated to Great Britain 1939

In 1947 Bělský was commissioned by the Czechoslovak Ministry of Defence to design the Paratroop Memorial in Prague and a medal in honour of Olympic athlete and long distance runner, Emil Zátopek. Zátopek first attracted international attention in 1946, as a private in the Czechoslovak army, when he bicycled from Prague to Berlin to enter the 5,000-metre race in an Allied Occupation Forces meet, which he subsequently won. He is best known for winning three gold medals at the 1952 Summer Olympics in Helsinki. Following this commission Bělský subsequently fled to England for the second time to escape from the Communist takeover of 1948. The medal is signed and dated "F. Bělský.48" and bears the embossed lettering: "ZÁTOPKŮV VOJENSKÝ ZÁVOD". It is illustrated in *Franta Bělský – Sculpture* published by Richter, Prague and A. Zwemmer Ltd., 1992.

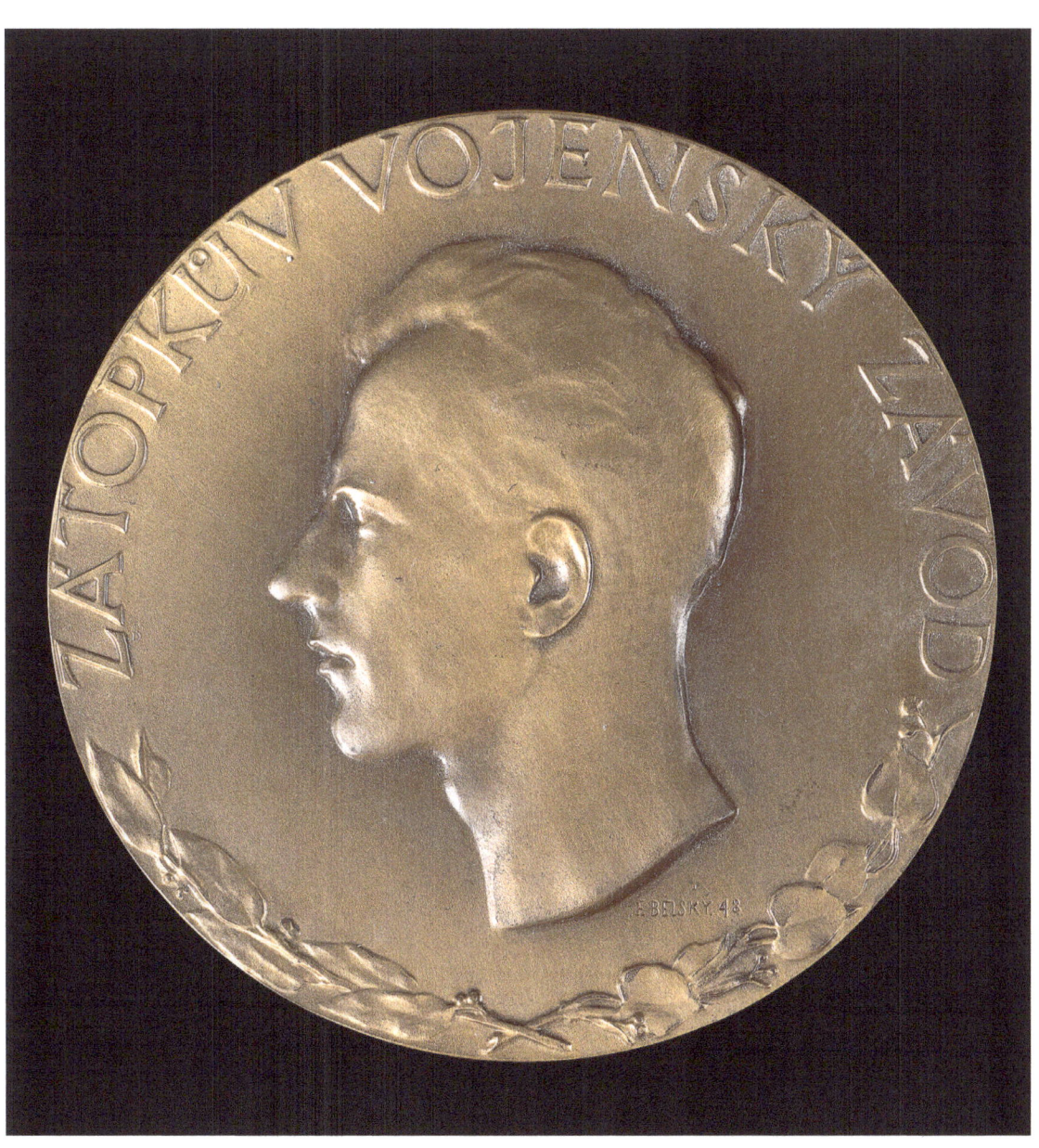

Emil Orlik

(1870, Prague, Czechoslovakia-1932, Berlin, Germany)

Head of a Man II

Lithograph on paper
23.4 x 19.9 cm

Ben Uri Collection

Portraitist and pioneering printmaker Emil Orlik was born into a Jewish family in Prague (then part of the Austro-Hungarian Empire) in 1870. The family was part of the large German-speaking community whose artistic circle included the writer Franz Kafka and poet Rainer Maria Rilke. Orlik drew from a young age and enrolled at the private art school of Heinrich Knirr, along with Paul Klee, before studying at the Munich Academy. He later learned engraving, experimented in printmaking techniques and became involved with the theatre as a leading set and costume designer. He spent most of 1898 travelling through Europe, visiting Great Britain – where he met the printmaker William Nicholson – and recorded his travels in numerous etchings, lithographs and woodcuts. In December 1917 Orlik was appointed official artist to the Brest-Litovsk Peace Conference at which

Russia and Germany ended their conflict and produced a number of portraits of Leon Trotsky. Portraiture makes up the majority of Orlik's oeuvre and includes depictions of artist friends as well as personalities from the worlds of theatre, music, literature, philosophy and science such as Oskar Kokoschka, Marc Chagall, Gustav Mahler and Henrik Ibsen. Such immediate, lightly executed lithographs are characteristic of most of the artist's later portrait albums, the technique enabling him to interpret his subjects with greater spontaneity. Orlik died of a heart attack in Berlin in 1932 and his brother Hugo inherited his estate, which included many paintings, drawings and prints by artists including Matisse and Cézanne. Hugo and his family perished during the war at the hands of the Nazis. The only survivor was an aunt who later regained some of Orlik's effects.

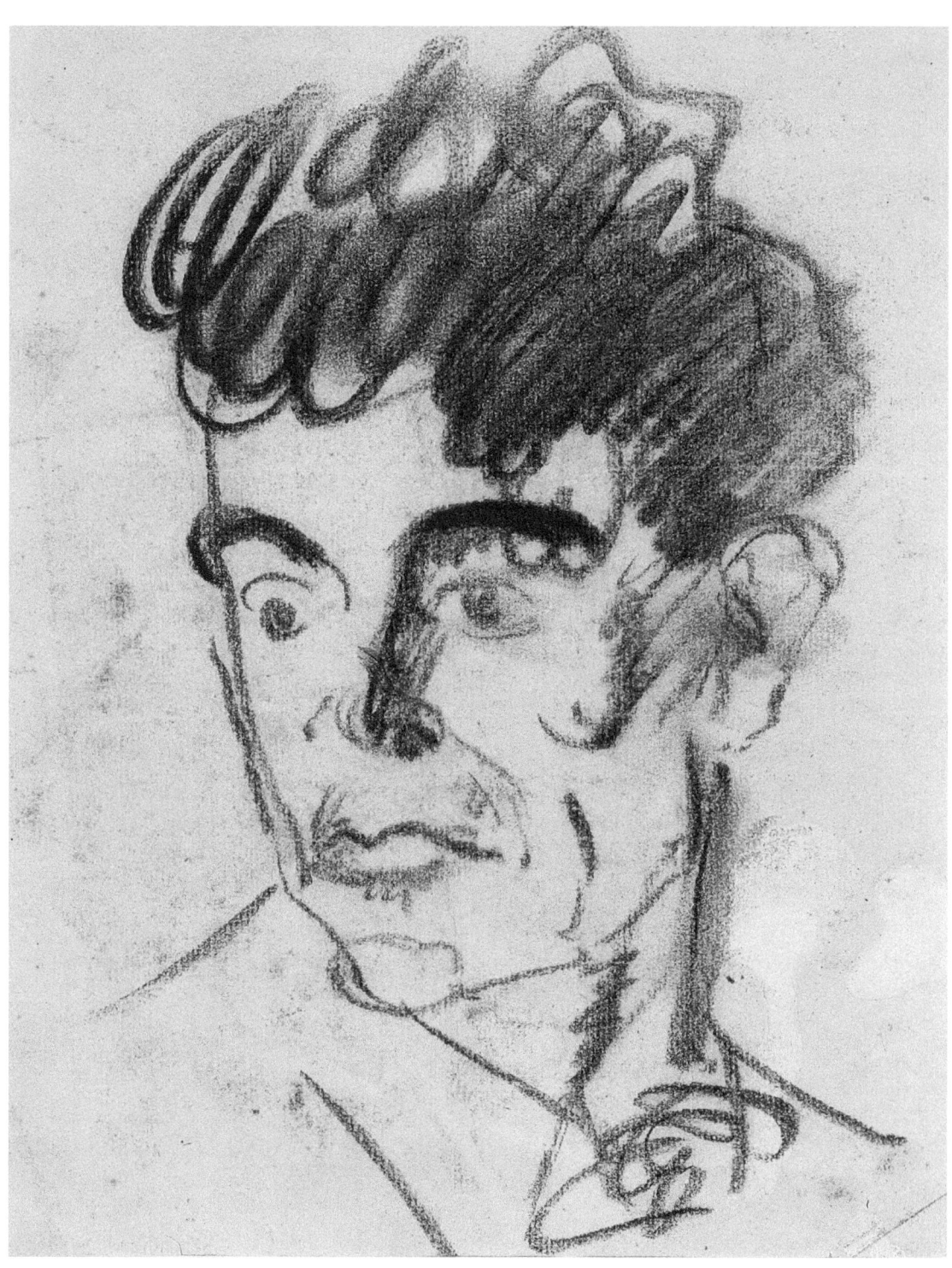

Walter Trier

(1890, Prague, Bohemia – 1951, Craigleith, Canada)

Market Woman

Pen and ink on paper
19 x 17.5 cm

Ben Uri Collection
Presented by Kurt Maschler

Immigrated to Great Britain 1936

Walter Trier was born in 1890 to German-Jewish parents in Prague, then the capital of a province within the Austro-Hungarian Empire. He trained briefly at the Prague Academy of Arts, Architecture and Design, before attending the Munich Academy in 1908, where he was taught by Franz von Stuck. Trier's illustrations were first published in 1909 in celebrated German satirical magazines *Simplicissimus* and *Jugend* (Youth), appearing alongside the work of well-known artists including Käthe Kollwitz and George Grosz. He became the regular press illustrator of Berlin based *Lustige Blätter* (Funny Pages) and within ten years was one of the most sought after cartoonists in Berlin. In 1929, Trier began a long standing working relationship with children's author Erich Kästner for whom he illustrated *Emil and the Detectives*, an instant sensation and literary classic. Following the rise of Nazism, he fled Germany with his family, settling in England in 1936. There he was able to continue working, designing in the region of 150 title pages for the humorous monthly magazine *Lilliput*, as well as illustrating anti-fascist pamphlets for the British Ministry of Information during the war. In 1947 Trier and his wife became British citizens, but followed their daughter to Ontario, Canada a few months later. This ludic and light-hearted example is characteristic of Trier's illustration work.

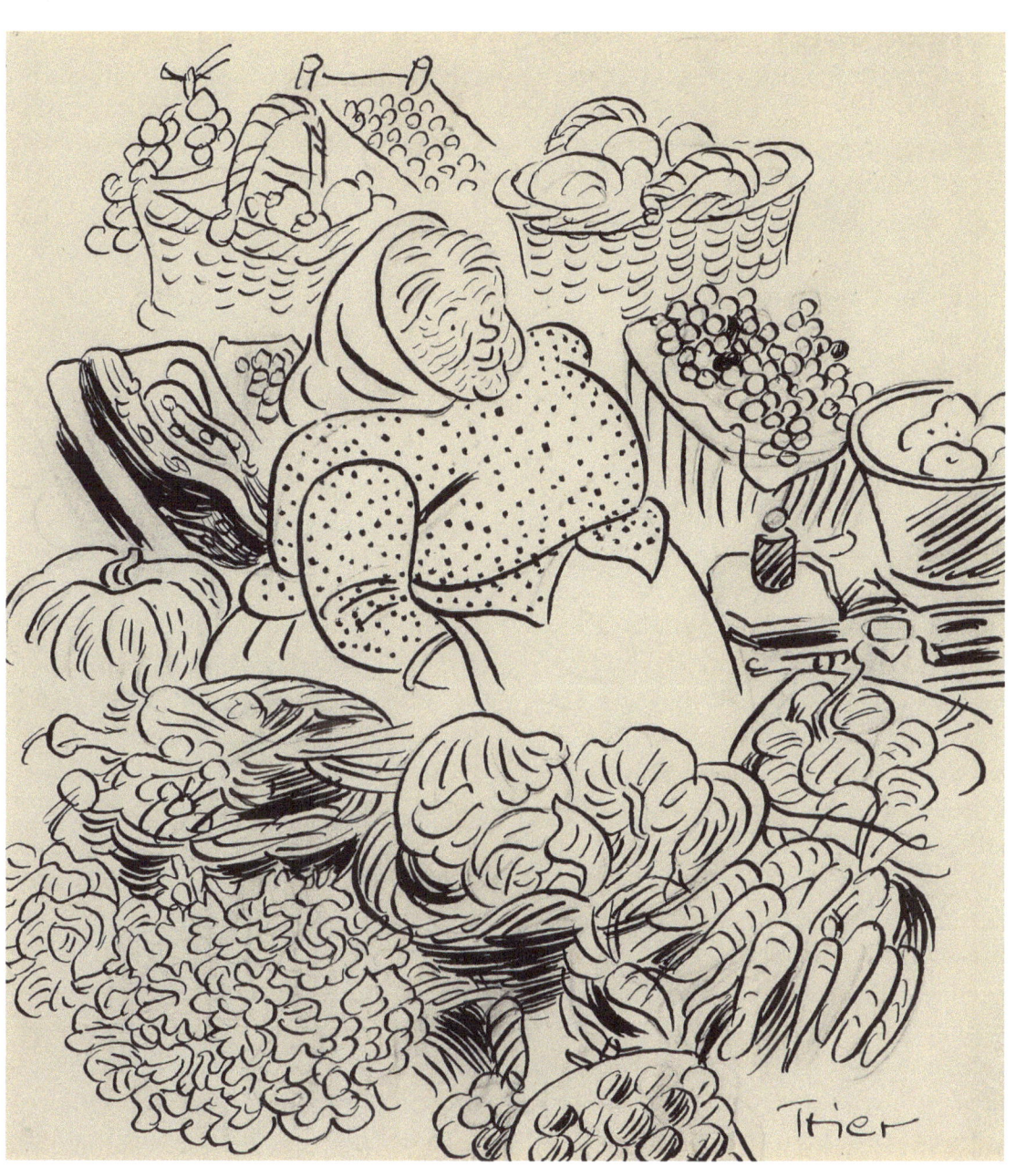

Bedřich Feigl

(Frederick, Friedrich, Fritz) (1884, Prague, Bohemia –1965, London, England)

The Restaurant

Gouache on paper
35 x 50.5 cm

Ben Uri Collection

Immigrated to Great Britain 1939

Painter Bedřich Feigl was born in Prague, then the capital of a province within the Austro-Hungarian Empire. Having studied briefly at the Academy of Arts in Prague, Feigl co-founded the group *Osma* which, in the words of Czechoslovak art historian J.P. Hodin, "strove ... to break with the dogma of the imitation of nature which reactionary Prague then demanded and to wrestle with the new problems of colour and form". Feigl travelled first to Antwerp then to Paris, afterwards living in Hamburg (1910) – establishing a significant reputation in Germany – and in Palestine (1932). He returned to Czechoslovakia in 1933 but fled in April 1939 after witnessing his country's occupation by the Nazis. Acting on advice from Oskar Kokoschka, who had known his gallerist brother Hugo well in Prague and who was already in England, Feigl requested help from the British Consulate in Cologne and was able to travel to London, settling first in Battersea then Highgate and finally in Hampstead. Although not featured in the *Entartete Kunst* exhibition of 1939 the Nazis considered Feigl's work 'degenerate'. It

was therefore confiscated and removed from public collections across Germany. In London his work was exhibited at the Czechoslovak Institute (1944) and most often within émigré circles including at Ben Uri (1959 and 1964), where he was also a member of the Arts Committee during the 1950s. Feigl returned repeatedly to the motif of coffee houses and restaurants, which he referred to as "the marketplaces of life". Attempting to recreate continental 'kaffe haus' culture in London, Feigl and others gathered at Cosmo, West Hampstead, where one could "spend all day reading [...] over a single cup of coffee or consuming Schnitzel and Strudel with fellow refugees". J. P. Hodin, with whom Feigl was by this time already close, promoted the intangible benefits of this café society in his published writings, while also pointing out the scarcity of such spaces in London: "[...] most of the modern principles in art and literature have been worked out over a sociable glass of wine or cup of coffee – in Paris, in Vienna, in Prague. But where does one meet these people in London?"

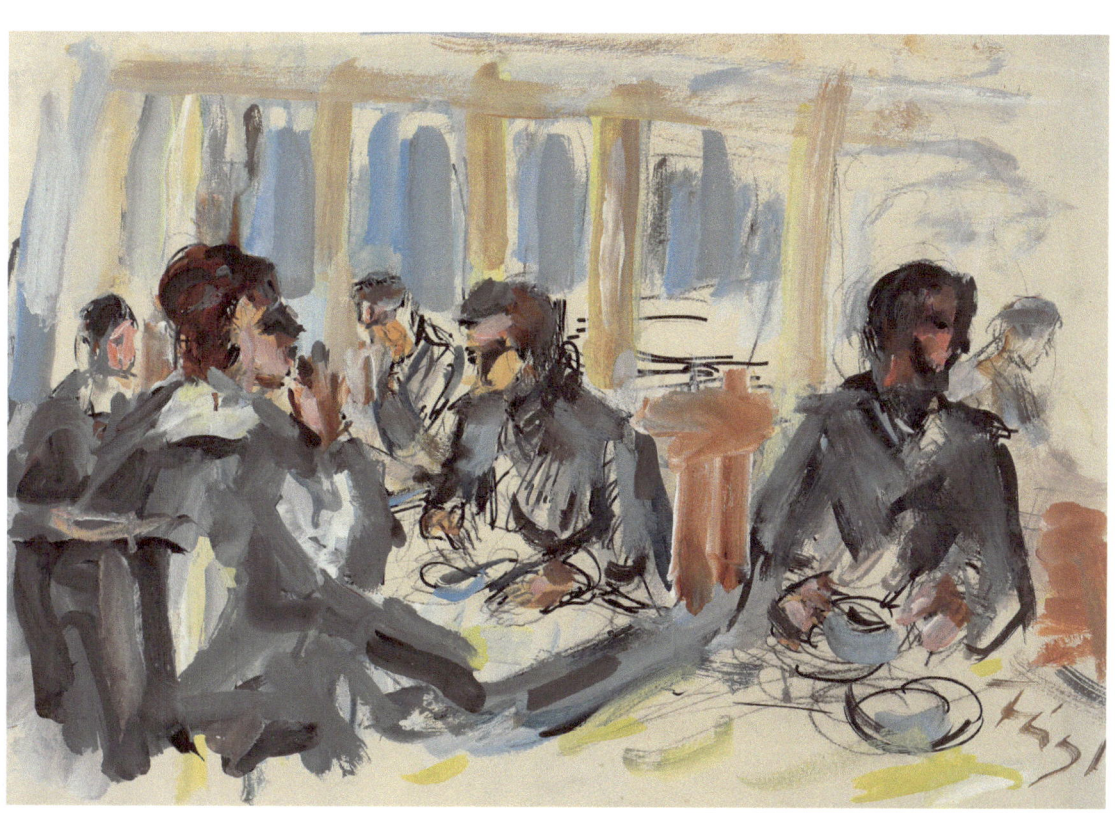

Irena Sedlecká
(1928, Pilsen, Czechoslovakia)

Sir John Gielgud in the role of Hamlet, 1993
Bronze
32.3 x 22.2 x 16.5cm
Signed and dated "I SEDLECKA" / "93", cast number "1 / 6"
with copyright mark and Pangolin Foundry mark

Private Collection

Immigrated to Great Britain 1966

The model for this sculpture is one of a series
of theatrical portraits, 'The Great Actors and
Singers', originally commissioned by actor
and collector Richard Bebb, others include
Laurence Olivier and Maria Callas. Eloquent
and expressive, this example was cast in hot
metal by Pangolin Editions foundry and
patinated with the approval of Irena Sedlecká.

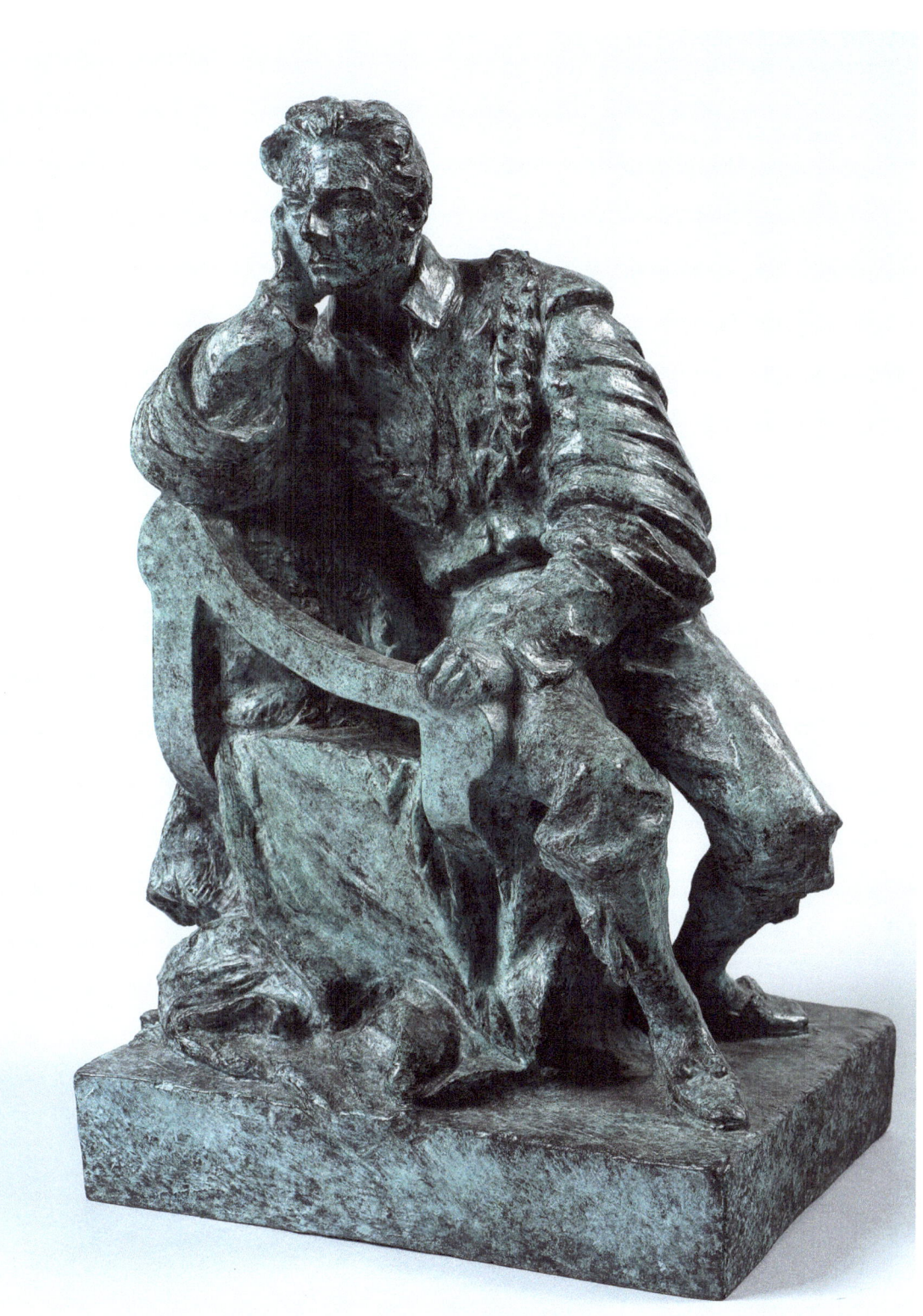

Irena Sedlecká

(1928, Pilsen, Czechoslovakia)

Kenneth Williams, 1981

Bronze
33 x 20 x 25.5cm
Signed "SEDLECKA" and cast number "1/3" with
Pangolin Foundry mark "PE" for Pangolin Edition

Private Collection

Immigrated to Great Britain 1966

A cast of this portrait of the comedic actor,
Kenneth Williams, was exhibited at the
Society of Portrait Sculptors, London, in
1981 and forms part of Sedlecká's extensive
'Talking Heads' series. A resin bronze cast
was subsequently exhibited in London by
the Society of Portrait Sculptors in *FACE
2000* (55) while this head was cast in bronze
shortly after 2000. Williams was one of the
main ensemble in 26 of the 31 *Carry On*
films, and appeared in many British television
programmes and radio comedies, including
a series with Tony Hancock and Kenneth
Horne. Other commissioned portrait heads
include Laurence Olivier, Donald Sinden, Paul
Eddington, Richard Briers, Jimmy Edwards,
Ted Moult, Bobby Charlton, Lord Litchfield
and Sir Frank Whittle.

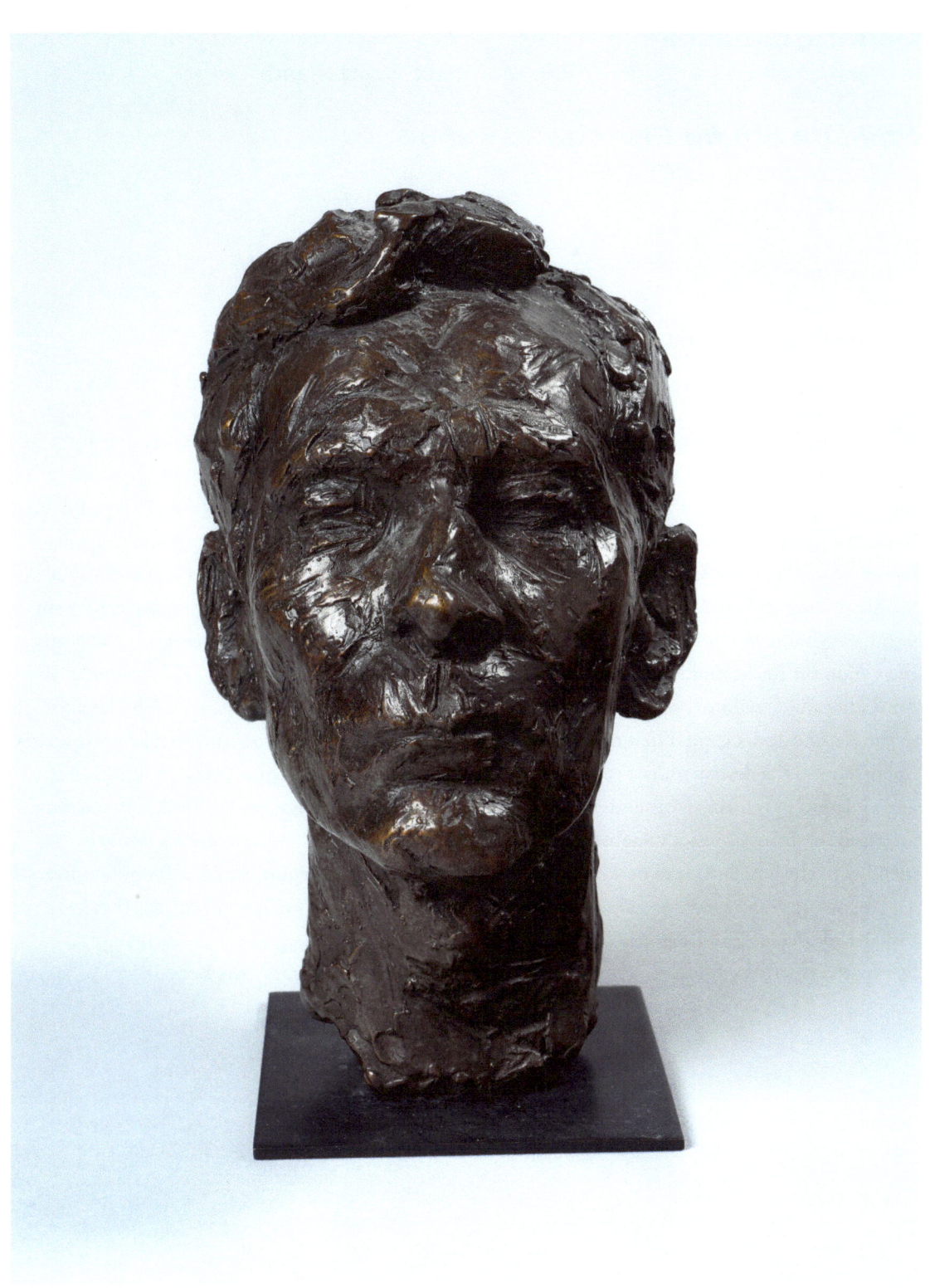

Oskar Kokoschka

(1886, Pöchlarn, Austria – 1980, Montreux, Switzerland)

Still-Life Studio Exercise, c. 1950

Watercolour on paper
63 x 47.5cm

Benjamin Midgley

Immigrated to Great Britain 1938, then Switzerland 1953

When violent political turmoil erupted in Vienna in 1934, Oskar Kokoschka seized the opportunity presented by a commission to paint a portrait of the President of Czechoslovakia Tomáš G. Masaryk, and moved to Prague. From 1935 onwards he wrote essays and gave speeches on behalf of the Union für Recht und Freiheit (Union for Rights and Freedom), an organisation in the Czechoslovak capital that mobilised opposition to the destruction of culture and violation of human rights and in 1936 attended the Brussels peace congress as a member of the Czechoslovak delegation. The following year he lent his name to the Oskar-Kokoschka-Bund, a group founded by expatriate artists who rejected the Nazis'

artistic ideals. Kokoschka fled Prague for England in 1938, the same year in which he had also gained Czechoslovak citizenship. He subsequently became a regular participant in the activities of the Free German League of Culture in London, advocating for Jewish emigrants and political enemies of the Nazis held in internment camps. This colourful and kinetic still life is dedicated to Charles and Regina Aukin, patrons of several émigré artists including Kokoschka, Jankel Adler and Lucy Rie. Both immigrants to London themselves, from Belarus and Germany respectively, Charles and Regina were life-long supporters of the Ben Uri Gallery. Charles' father Dov Aukin was a cosignatory to the inaugural meeting establishing the Ben Uri in 1915.

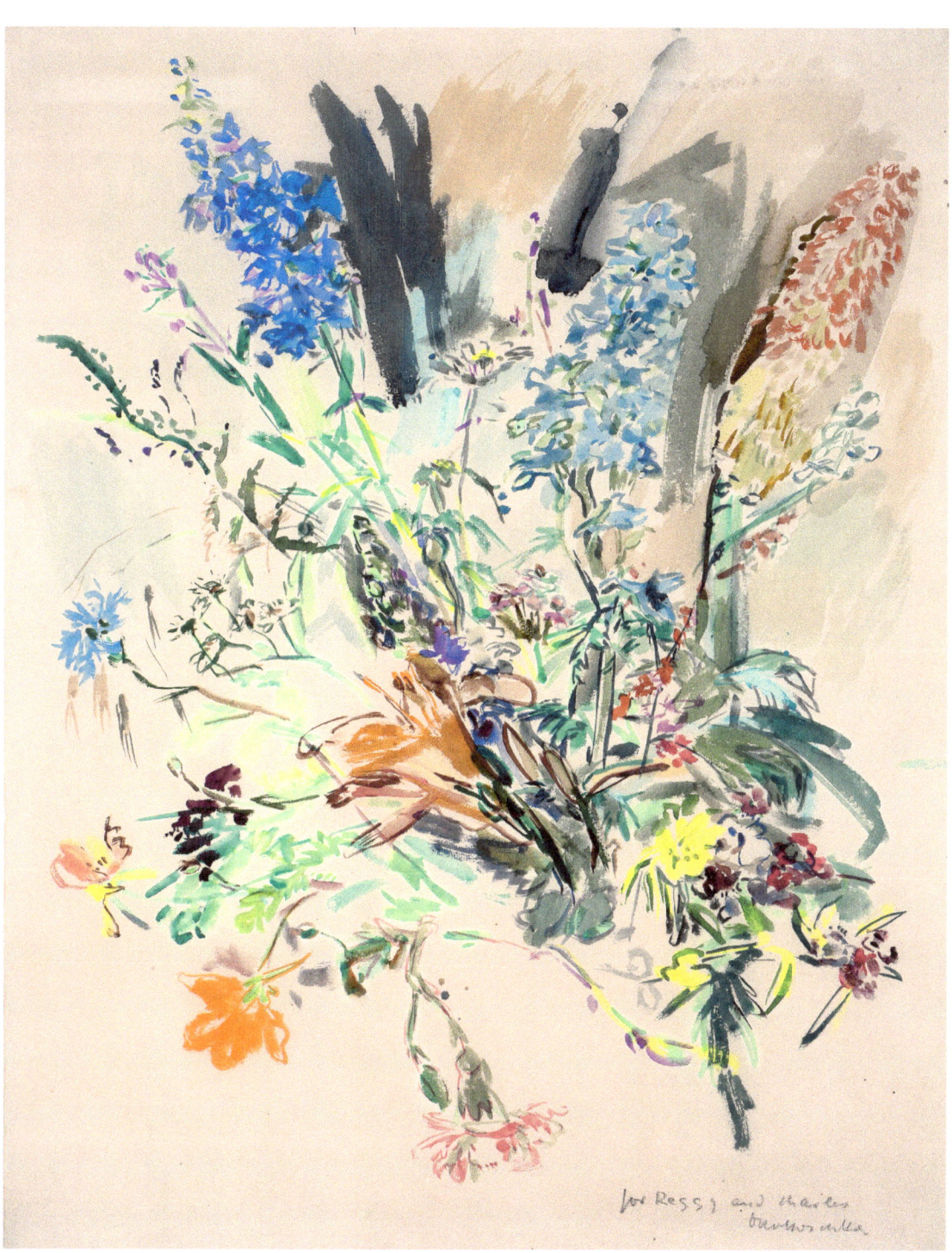

for Ress; and Charles
Oskoswalka

Oskar Kokoschka

(1886 Pöchlarn, Austria – 1980, Montreux, Switzerland)

The Donkey

Coloured Chalks on paper
20 x 30cm
Inscribed to Pamela Hodin – 'the beautiful one'
Private Collection

Immigrated to Great Britain 1938, then Switzerland 1953

The Donkey is one of several works made for
the eminent Czech émigré art historian J. P.
Hodin (1905–1995), author of a Kokoschka
monograph (1966), and affectionately
dedicated to Hodin's wife Pamela.

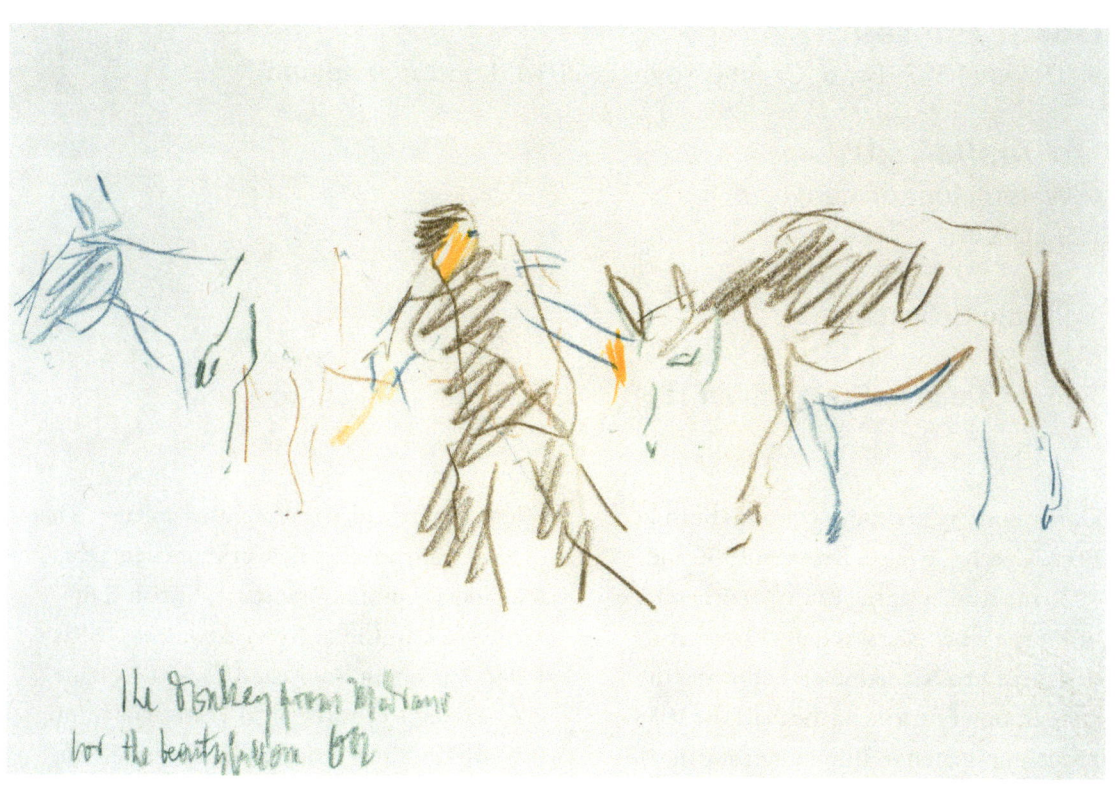

The Donkey from Medame
for the beauty party 6/12

Dorrit Epstein,

(Dekk) (1917, Brno, Czechoslovakia-2014, London, England)

'To Tasha', 2010

Watercolour on card
9 x 16cm

Private Collection

Immigrated to Great Britain 1938

Dorrit Epstein, née Fuhrmann was born in Brno, Czechoslovakia. Between 1936 and 1938 she studied at the Kunstgewerbeschule in Vienna where she was taught by stage designer Otto Niedermoser. Following the annexation of Austria by the Nazis in 1938, Dekk immigrated to Britain, settling in London where she took up a scholarship at the Reimann School, specialising in graphic design. She then joined the Women's Royal Naval Service (WRNS) and as a linguist became a radio intelligence officer intercepting coded messages sent to German naval forces. After the war she adopted the professional name of *Dekk* and joined the design studio of what was to become the Central Office of Information, producing numerous posters – for the Ministry of Health and Ministry of Works. A great admirer of the photomontagist,

John Heartfield, she often used collage in her design and advertising work for clients that included London Transport, British Rail and the Post Office Savings Bank as well as P&O, Penguin Books and Tatler magazine. As a designer for the 1951 Festival of Britain's Land Travelling Exhibition she created the mural 'British Sports and Games', subsequently displayed in cities across the Midlands and the north of England. In 1956, she became a Fellow of the Society of Industrial Artists. She retired from her graphic design practice in 1982, but continued to work as a painter and printmaker up until her death in December 2014. *To Tasha* is a birthday card and thus not intended for public display, but is characteristic of Dekk's carefree, colourful work.

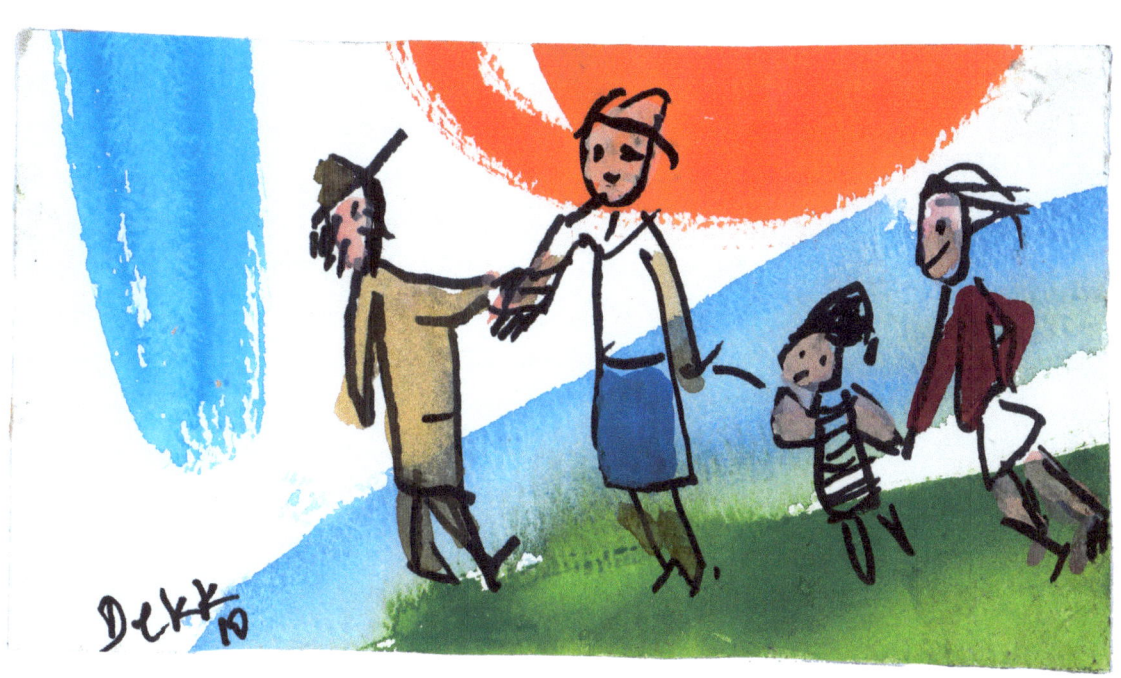

Tereza Bušková

(1978, Prague, Czechoslovakia)

Erdingtonia, 2016

Digital inkjet archival prints with two colour (metallic gold) overlay on Somerset satin paper

15 x 21cm

Property of the artist

Immigrated to Great Britain 1998

Multi-disciplinary artist, Tereza Bušková (b.1978, Prague) lives and works in Birmingham. Following a BA in Fine Art Bušková completed an MA in Fine Art Printmaking at the Royal College of Art in 2007. Bušková's practice deals with ritual, tradition and craft, celebrating and reinterpreting Slavic as well as European customs through the media of print, performance and video. The *Clipping the Church* series sought to revive an ancient and almost forgotten English tradition as part of which families would flock to local churches, holding hands with each other in order to encircle it with open arms. Bušková reflects that, "As a Czech immigrant it struck me as a great way to literally bring people together to celebrate". More than 200 people were present at the artist's orchestrated re-enactment of the clipping of St Barnabus Church, Erdington, Birmingham in June 2016, 13 days prior to the Brexit referendum. As a potent symbol of identity and belonging, such a public art project united a disparate community. These prints, produced as if they were postcards of the mythical town of Erdingtonia, a place where leave voters and EU migrants live hand in hand, commemorate the clipping of the church by combining Bohemian wedding celebrations with English rituals.

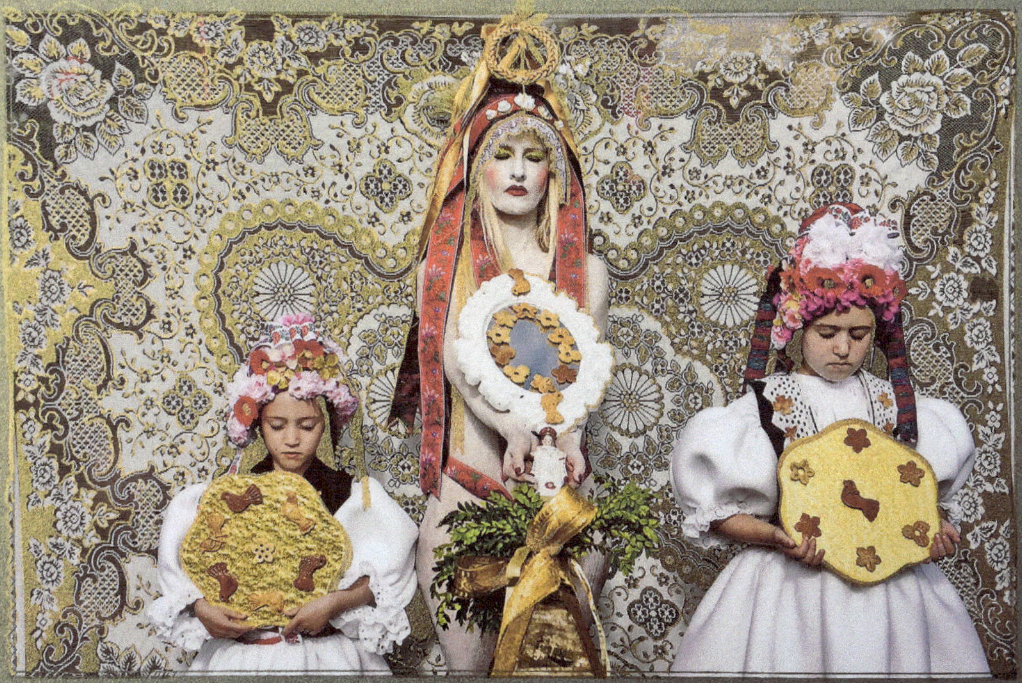

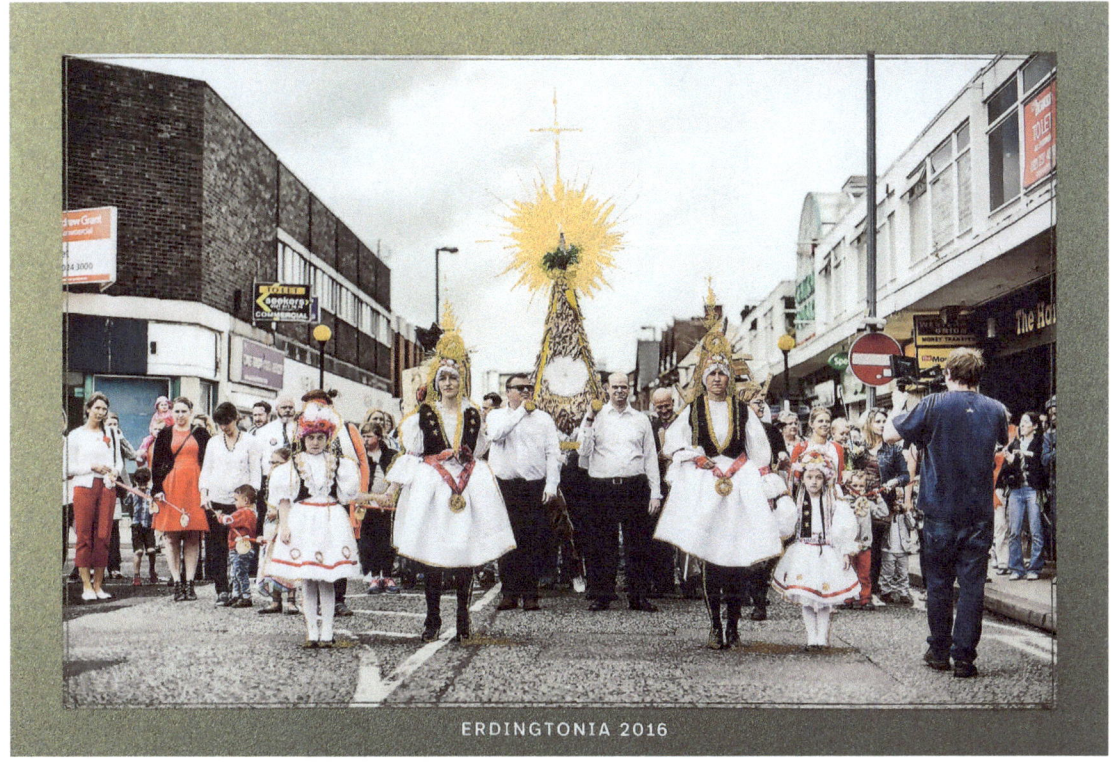

ERDINGTONIA 2016

ERDINGTONIA 2016

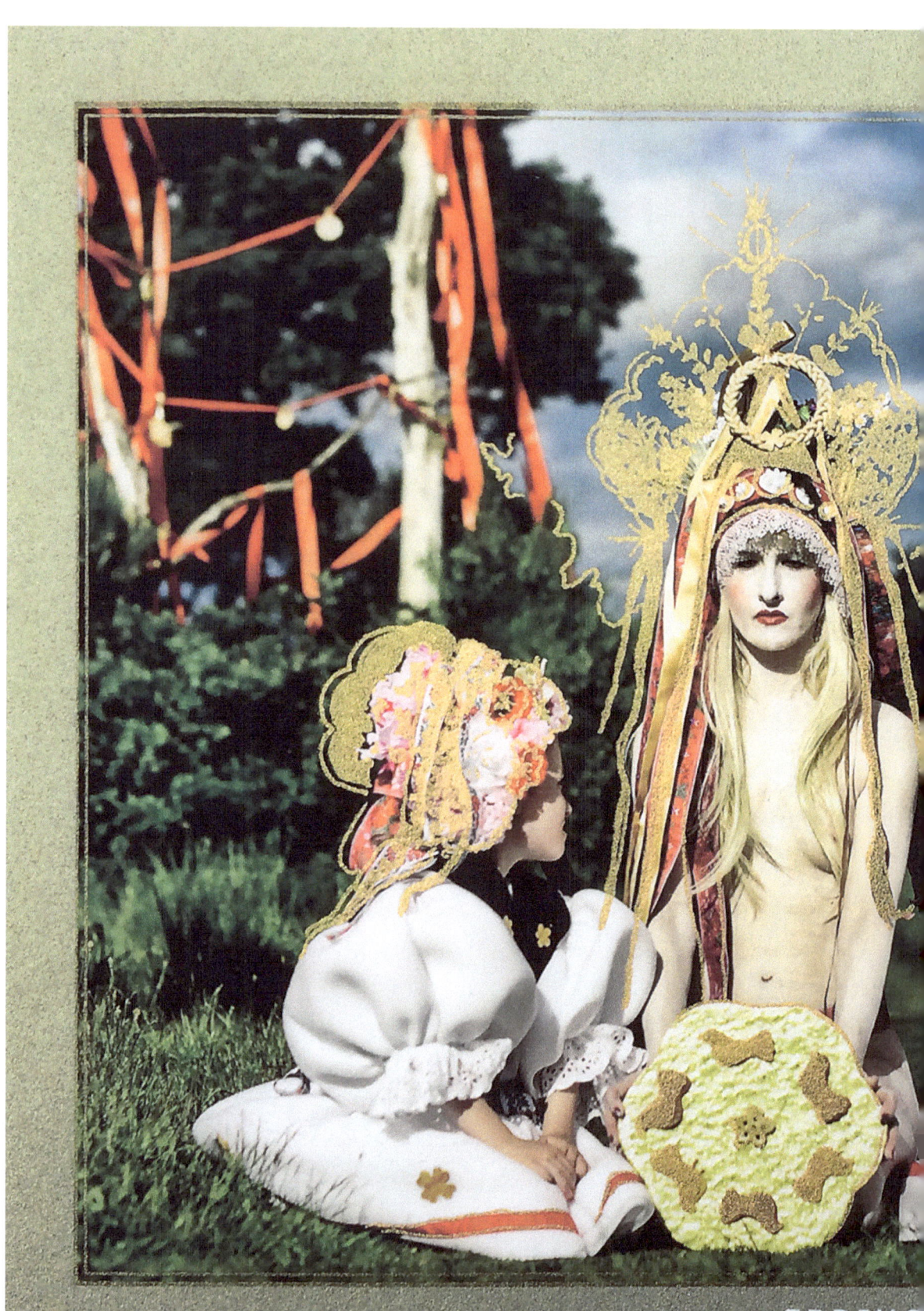

ERDING

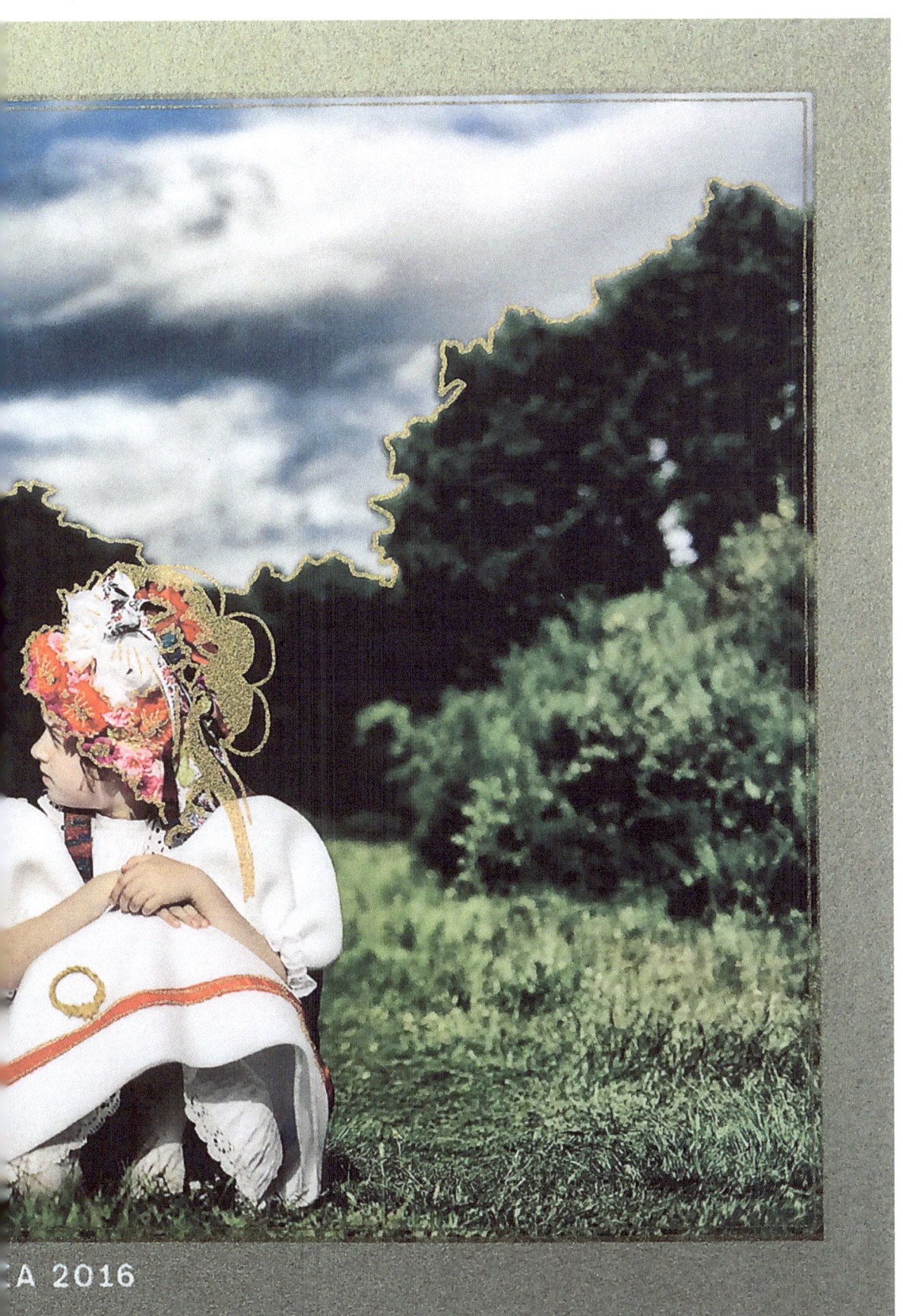

A 2016

Mila Fürstová
(1975, Pelhřimov, Czechoslovakia)

Town Tree, 2012
Etching on paper
34 x 34cm

Property of the artist

Immigrated to Great Britain 1996

Born in Czechoslovakia, Mila Fürstová (b. 1975, Pelhřimov) holds a BA in Fine Art Printmaking, an MA in Art, English Language and Psychology from Charles University in Prague and an MA from the Royal College of Art. In 2003, she was appointed the first Artist in Residence at Cheltenham Ladies' College, where she founded and ran an Etching studio and in 2009 she became the youngest member of The Royal West of England Academy. Inspired by "universal and personal mythologies", her work is "an intimate portrayal of the human soul explored through the medium of etching and expressed in a distinctly female voice, which she describes

as, 'urgent, fragile yet strong, gentle yet enquiring". In the artist's own words "I cut, fold and overlay my works, often printing on glass or other transparent surfaces thus creating imagery that is multidimensional in terms of both form and meaning. The technique of etching uniquely reflects and informs the spirit of my work. I draw with a needle onto a plate, allowing the image to quietly grow, whilst a fragile silver line emerges from a dark background as if a distant memory was traced from the unconscious". Both *Town Tree,* in its depiction, perhaps, of the artist's Czech roots, and *Nest* resonate too with the themes of identity and migration and belonging.

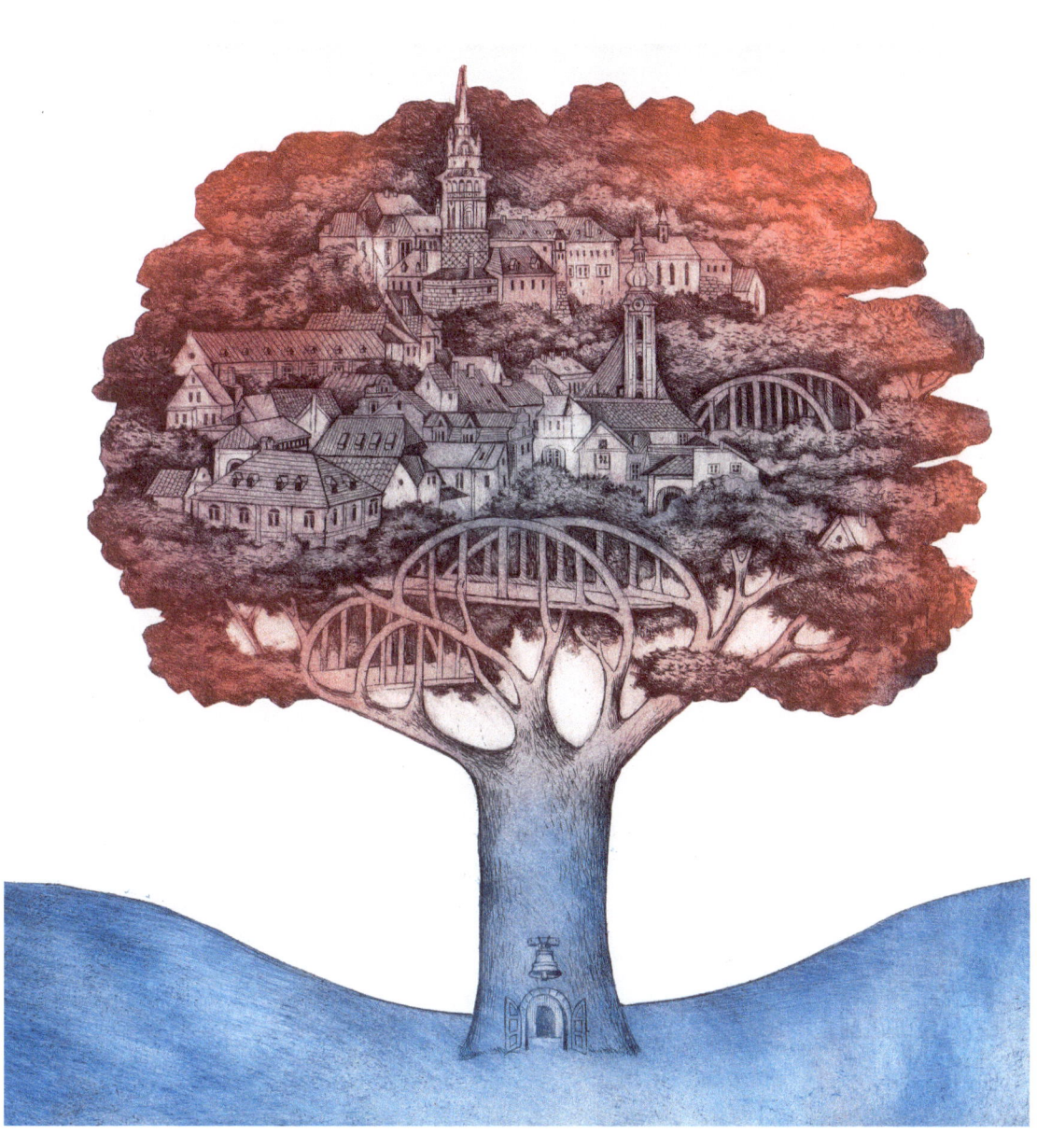

Mila Fürstová

(1975, Pelhřimov, Czechoslovakia)

Nest, 2011

Etching on paper
56 x 42cm

Property of the artist

Immigrated to Great Britain 1996

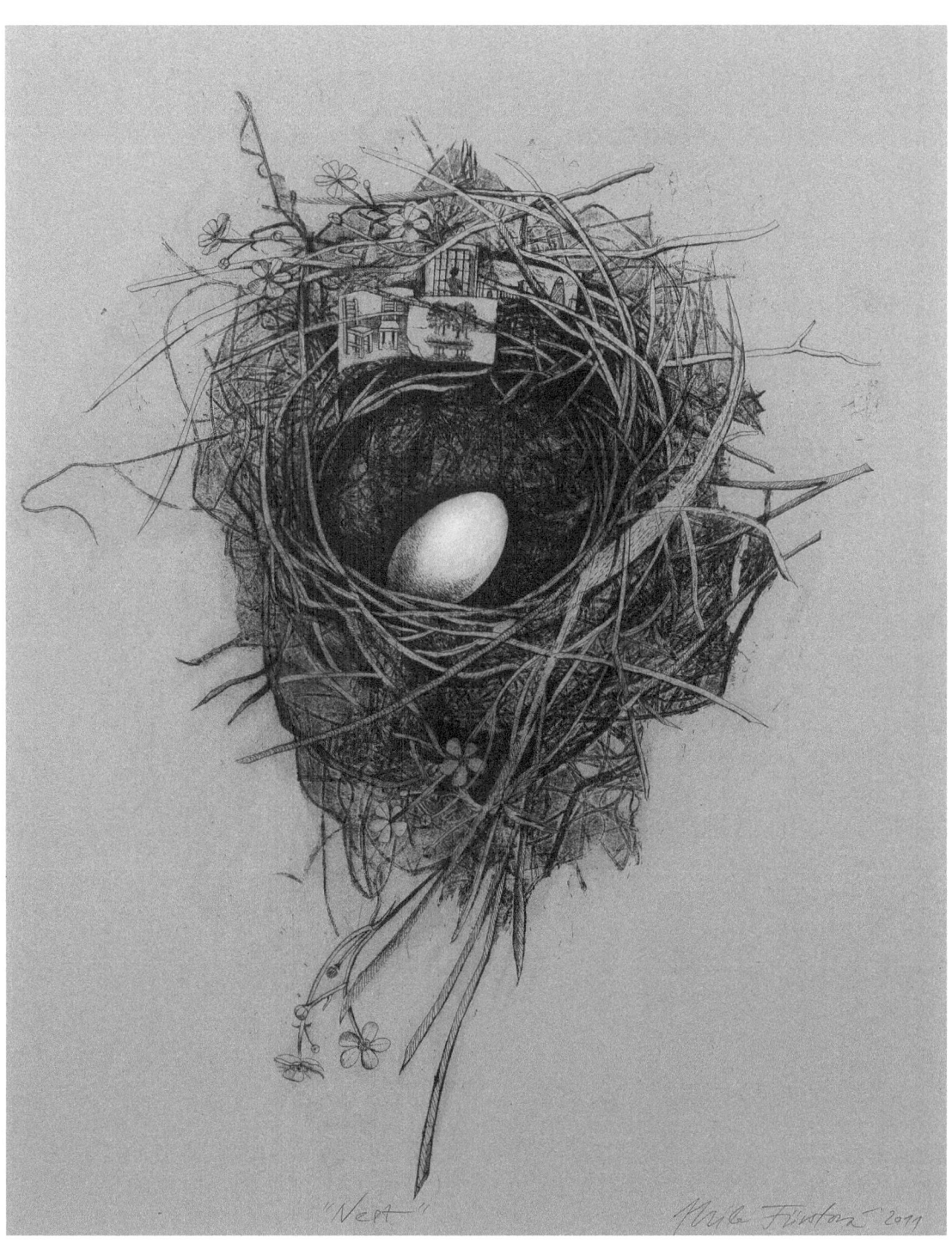

"Nest"   Mike Fortons 2011

Tereza Stehlíková

(1975, Prague)

Railtracks, 2013

Book

Property of the artist

Immigrated to Great Britain 1991

Tereza Stehlíková, (b. 1975, Prague) holds a PhD from the Royal College of Art, where she researched the tactile language of film. She is currently engaged in a cross-disciplinary research, exploring how moving images can be used to capture and communicate multi-sensory experiences and embodied memory. Stehliková is a senior lecturer at the University of Westminster and a research coordinator at the RCA. She is also a founding member of *Sensory Sites*, an international collective generating collaborative exhibitions and research projects that explore sensory perception and bodily experience. *Railtracks* is a collaboration between writers, John Berger and Anne Michaels, a sensual and exploratory dialogue illustrated throughout by photographs taken by Stehlíková which chart an atmospheric journey by train through the winter landscapes of Southern Bohemia.

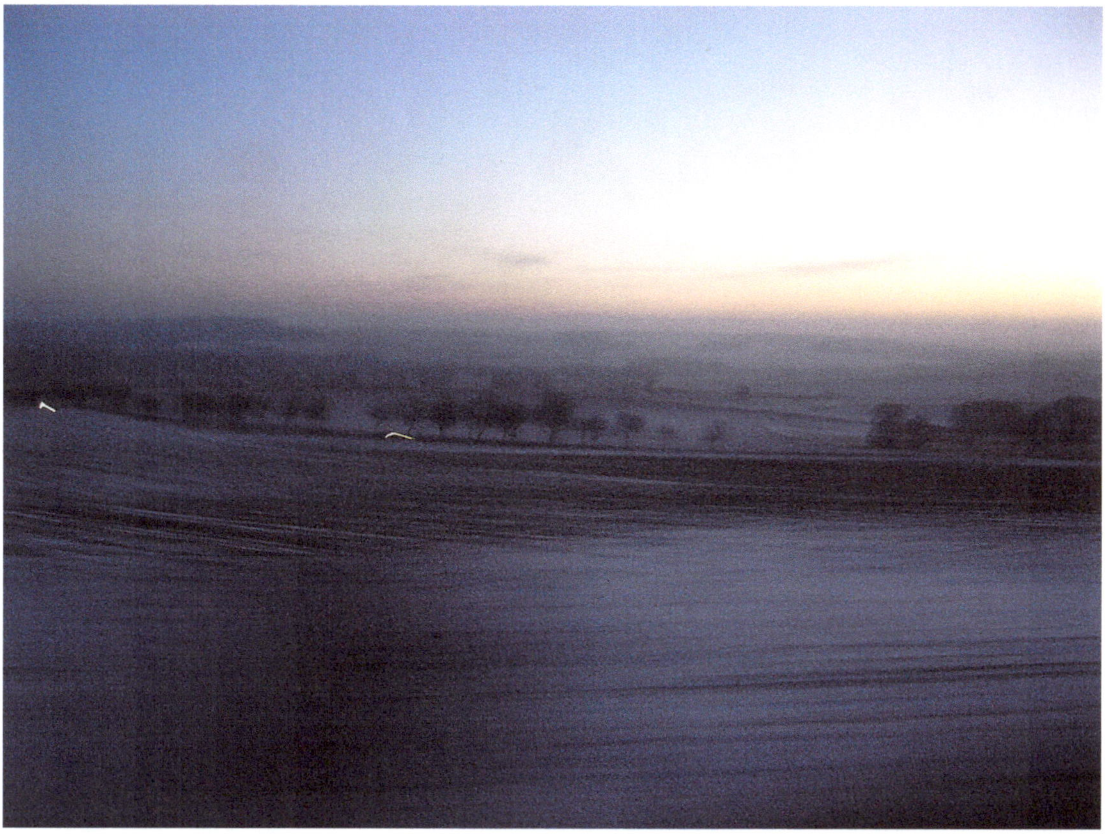

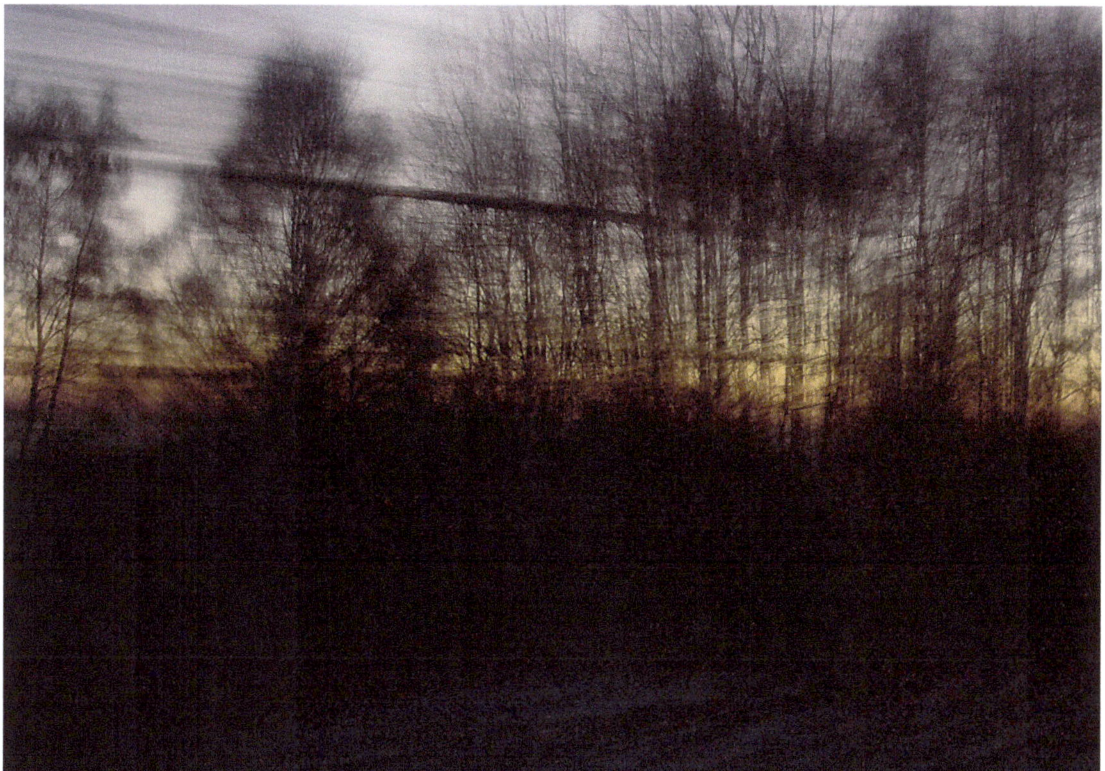

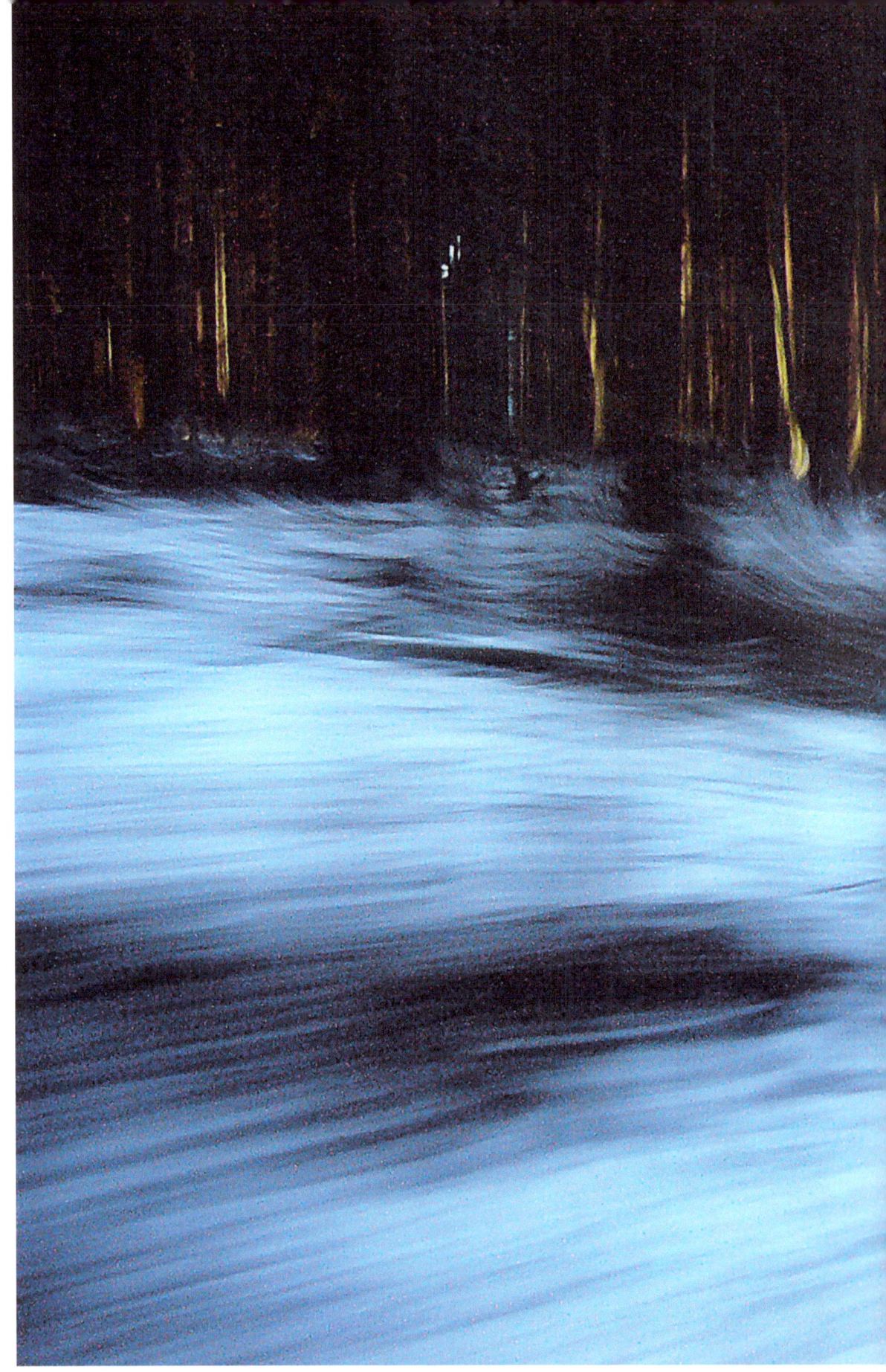

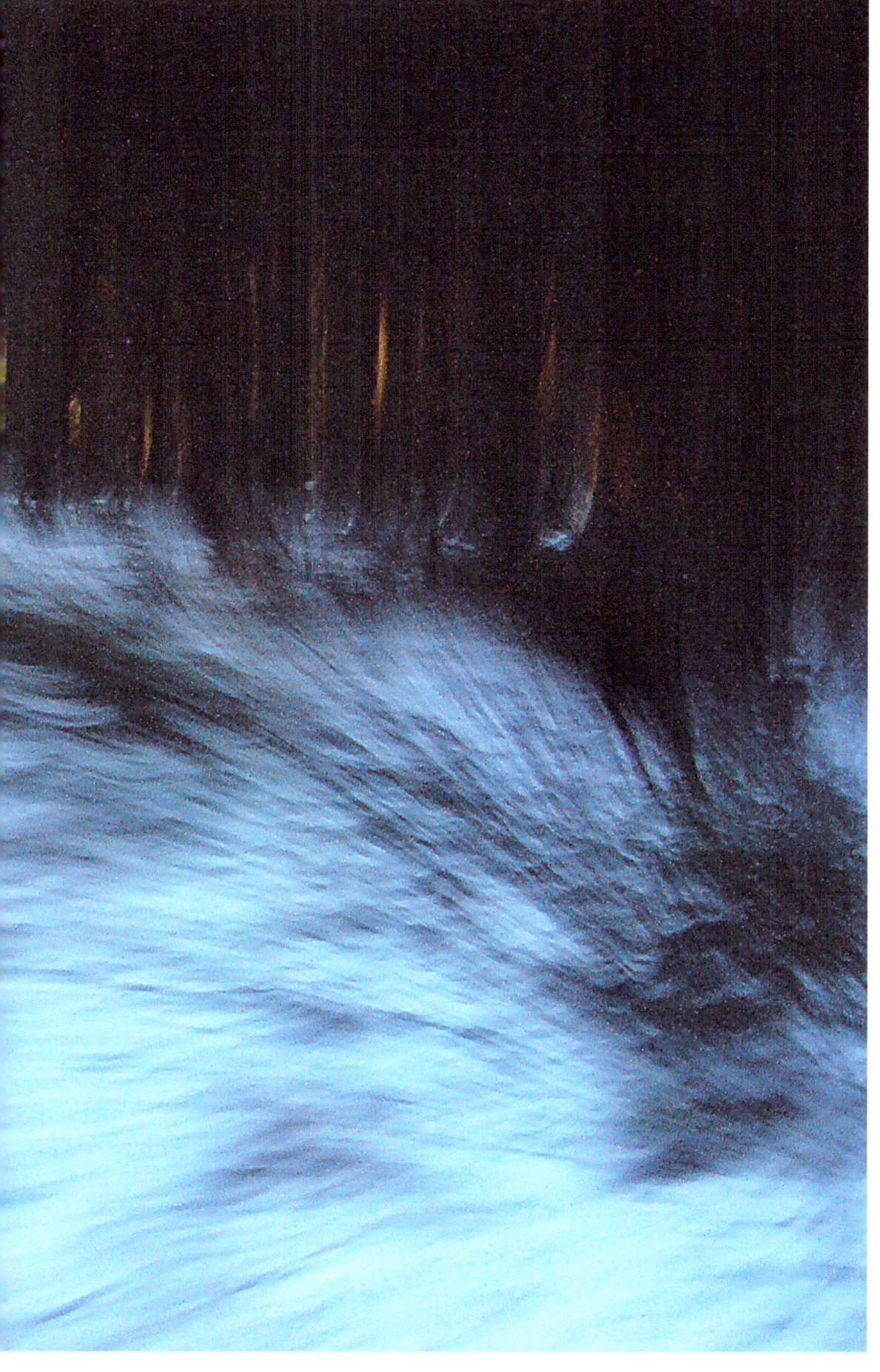

Timeline including selected exhibitions

1898 – Emil Orlik travels within Europe, visiting Great Britain, where he meets the printmaker William Nicholson

1915 – Ben Uri Society founded in Whitechapel

1918 – With the collapse of the Austro-Hungarian Empire, the independent country of Czechoslovakia was formed – a merger of the lands of the Bohemian Crown, Slovakia, and Carpathian Ruthenia

1919 – The Czechoslovak Colony Club is established by World War I legionnaires in Gloucester Avenue, north London.

1925 – Ben Uri opens its first gallery in Great Russell Street, Bloomsbury

1936 – Walter Trier flees Germany with his family, immigrating to Great Britain

1938 – The Sudetenland, Czechoslovakia's northern frontier is ceded to Hitler under the terms of the Munich Agreement (29th September)
 The British Committee for Refugees from Czechoslovakia (BCRC) is formed, subsequently becoming the Czech Refugee Trust Fund, and is responsible for refugees from Czechoslovakia whilst remaining answerable to both the Treasury and the Secretary of State for the Home Department.
 Freda Salvendy flees Vienna, immigrating to Great Britain
 Dorrit Dekk flees Vienna, immigrating to Great Britain
 John Heartfield flees Prague, immigrating to Great Britain with the help of the British Committee for Refugees from Czechoslovakia (later named Czech Refugee Trust Fund)
 Oskar Kokoschka flees Prague having gained Czechoslovak citizenship, immigrating to Great Britain

1939 – Hitler invades 'rump'
Czechoslovakia (15th March). Outbreak
of the Second World War
Jacob Bornfriend flees Prague,
immigrating to Great Britain
Bedřich Feigl flees Prague, immigrating
to Great Britain
Walter Herz flees Czechoslovakia,
immigrating to Great Britain
Käthe Strenitz escapes Czechoslovakia,
travelling on a Quaker sponsored
Kindertransport to England
Anita Mandl escapes Czechoslovakia,
travelling on a Quaker sponsored
Kindertransport to Great Britain
Leo Haas is arrested and sent into
forced labour
Dorrit Dekk joins the Women's Royal
Naval Service (WRNS) and intercepts
coded messages sent to German naval
forces, her handwritten transcripts are
sent to Bletchley Park for deciphering
Franta Bělský flees Prague, immigrating
to Great Britain
By December some 12,000 refugees
from Czechoslovakia are resident
in Britain

1940 – Czechoslovak forces in the UK
officially formed at Cholmondeley Park

1940-45 – Britain hosts President Beneš
and the Czechoslovak Government
in Exile

1941 – The exhibition *Three Czechs:
Bedřich Feigl, Freda Salvendy, Karel
Vogel* is held at the Leicester Museum
and Art Gallery, Leicester
The Czechoslovak Institute at 18
Grosvenor Place, London is formally
opened by Anthony Eden, Secretary of
State for Foreign Affairs in January
The Communist inspired Czechoslovak-
British Friendship Club opens
in September

1940s – Käthe Strenitz commits to war
work, making air force goggles and
moves into the Czech Refugee Trust
Fund-maintained Canterbury Hall hostel
Geza Szobel joins the Czechoslovak
Army in France and subsequently
immigrates to Great Britain

1942 – Geza Szobel's series *Civilisation* is
exhibited at the Czechoslovak Institute
and the V&A in London alongside
Goya's *Los Desastres de la Guerra* and
Jacques Callot's *Les Misères et Malheurs
de la Guerre*. The series is also published
by Penguin Books.

1942-43 – Yehuda Bacon is deported to
Terezín and subsequently to Auschwitz

1942-45 – Leo Haas is deported to
Terezín and subsequently to Auschwitz
and Sachsenhausen

1943 – 1st Czechoslovak Armoured Brigade formed and subsequently transferred to northern France and used to lay siege to the isolated German garrison in Dunkirk. It remained there until a few days after the end of hostilities in May 1945

1943-44 – Shraga Weil and his wife are arrested and sent to a concentration camp and then to prison, from which they escape.

1944 – Bedřich Feigl's work is exhibited at the Czechoslovak Institute, London

1945 – Yehuda Bacon is liberated from Mauthausen
Leo Haas is liberated by the Americans from Ebensee
Jacob Bornfriend's work is exhibited at the Czechoslovak Institute, London

1946 – Freda Salvendy's *Prague* is exhibited at the Ben Uri Gallery

1947 – Walter Trier and his wife become British citizens; his work is exhibited at the Ben Uri Gallery

1948 – Communist coup in Czechoslovakia
Walter Herz designs the official poster for the London Olympic Games

Late 1940s – Yehuda Bacon spends a year in London studying at the Central School of Arts and Crafts
The Czech and Slovak Bar and Restaurant opens on West End Lane in West Hampstead

1951 – As a designer for the 1951 Festival of Britain's Land Travelling Exhibition Dekk creates the mural 'British Sports and Games', subsequently displayed in cities across the Midlands and the North of England.

1956 – Dorrit Dekk becomes a Fellow of the Society of Industrial Artists.

1957 – Jacob Bornfriend is commissioned to design a mural for Jews' College, London
Yehuda Bacon's work is exhibited in a solo show at the Ben Uri Gallery

1959 – Bedřich Feigl's work is exhibited in a solo show at the Ben Uri Gallery

1961 – Käthe Strenitz's paintings are exhibited in a solo show at the Ben Uri Gallery

1962 – Shraga Weil's work is exhibited at the Ben Uri Gallery

1964 – Bedřich Feigl's work is exhibited in a solo show at the Ben Uri Gallery to celebrate his 80th birthday

1966 – Irena Sedlecká flees Prague, immigrating to Great Britain

1967 – Leo Haas's work is exhibited at the Ben Uri Gallery

1968 – A period of political liberalisation known as the Prague Spring is forcibly ended when five Warsaw Pact member countries invade Czechoslovakia; Soviet troops continue to occupy the country until 1989

1974 – Jacob Bornfriend's work is exhibited at the Ben Uri Gallery Scarlet Nikolska leaves Prague, immigrating to Great Britain

1975 – Scarlet Nikolska has a solo show at the Ben Uri Gallery

1989 – The Velvet Revolution brings an end to communism in Czechoslovakia

1990 – The British Czech and Slovak Association (BCSA) is launched by Alexander Dubcek in November with the aim of raising awareness of matters relating to the history, arts, literature, politics, economies and science of Britain and the Czech and Slovak Republics

1991 – Tereza Stehlíková leaves Prague, immigrating to Great Britain

1993 – Czechoslovakia peacefully splits into two countries, the Czech Republic and Slovakia
The Czech Centre London opens. It is a non-political organisation supported by the Czech Ministry of Foreign Affairs as part of a worldwide network of 21 Czech Centres operating in 19 countries and on three continents.

1996 – Mila Fürstová leaves Prague, immigrating to Great Britain

1998 – Tereza Bušková leaves Prague, immigrating to Great Britain

Czech Jewish Artists from the Collection exhibited at Ben Uri Gallery

2004 – Czech Republic and Slovakia are two of ten new nations to join the EU

2009 – Mila Fürstová becomes the youngest member of The Royal West of England Academy

2011-2013 – Tereza Stehlíková collaborates with John Berger and Anne Michaels on *Railtracks*, a dialogue illustrated throughout by photographs taken by Stehlíková of wintery Southern Bohemia.

2013 – It is estimated that 45,000 Czech-born immigrants are resident in the U.K.

2015 – Ben Uri celebrates its centenary with an exhibition at Somerset House, London.

2016 – Tereza Bušková orchestrates
the 'clipping' of St Barnabus
Church, Birmingham
Tereza Stehliková makes a short
film, *Trieste: In-between states*, an
impressionistic documentary inspired
by a conversation with John Berger
and intertwined with excerpts
from Deborah Levy's short story,
Swallowing Geography.

2018 – It is estimated that 60,000 Slovaks
are resident in the U.K.

2019 – *Czech Routes: Selected
Czechoslovak Artists in Britain from the
Ben Uri and Private Collections* exhibited
at the Ben Uri Gallery and Museum

Select Bibliography

Bělský, Franta, *Sculpture*, (Richter, Prague and A. Zwemmer Ltd., London, 1992)

Brinson, Charmian ed., *Exile in and from Czechoslovakia during the 1930s and 1940s* (Amsterdam: Rodopi, 2009)

Burešová, Jana Barbora, *London's Czechoslovak Institute during World War II*, 27th March 2019, Research Centre for German and Austrian Exile Studies, Institute for Modern Languages Research, University of London. Lecture.

Burstow, Robert, 'Institutional patronage of central and eastern European émigré sculptors in Britain c1945 – 1965: Moderate modernism for the social-democratic consensus', *The British Art Journal*, Vol. XIX, No.3, Winter 2018/2019, pp.38-47

Cannon-Brookes, Peter, *Czech Sculpture 1800-1938* (London: Trefoil Books, 1983)

Dickson, Rachel and Sarah MacDougall, 'Fred Feigl in England: "Modern Art is a Sputnik"', *Friedrich Feigl*, ed. by Nicholas Sawicki (Prague: Arbor, Vitae, 2017)

Hahn F., 'Czechoslovakia and the Anti-Hitler Emigrants, 1933–39', in: Kirschbaum S.J. ed., *Historical Reflections on Central Europe*, International Council for Central and East European Studies (London: Palgrave Macmillan, 1999)

Parik, Arno, *Emil Orlik: Portraits of Friends and Contemporaries*, (Prague: Jewish Museum, 2004)

Petrasová, Taťána, and Rostislav Švácha eds., *Art in the Czech Lands 8000-2000*, The Institute of Art History, Czech Academy of Sciences, (Prague: Abor Vitae, 2017)

Szobel, Geza, *Civilisation*, (London: Penguin, 1942)

Snowman, Daniel, *Hitler Emigrés: The Cultural Impact on Britain of Refugees from Nazism* (London: Chatto & Windus, 2002)

Tieze, Agnes, ed., *Oskar Kokoschka and the Prague Cultural Scene* (Köln: Wienand Verlag, 2016)

Vinzent, Jutta and Jennifer Powell, *Identity and Image: Refugees from Nazi Germany in Britain 1933-45* (Kromsdorf/Weimar: VDG, 2005)

The Atelier Sale of Franta Bělský and Irena Sedlecká (Oxford: Mallams, 25th April 2017)

Contributor Biographies

Nicola Baird is a Research Officer at the Ben Uri Research Unit (BURU). Other recent projects have included co-curating an Arts Council funded retrospective of the work of German émigré artist, Fred Uhlman at Burgh House & Hampstead Museum in 2018, which toured to Hatton Gallery, Newcastle later that year. She is a PhD candidate at London South Bank University co-sponsored by the University and by Ben Uri Gallery and Museum.

Dr. Peter Cannon-Brookes studied Natural Sciences at Cambridge (MA) and History of Art at The Courtauld Institute of Art, London University (PhD). He was Keeper of the Departments of Art, City Museum and Art Gallery, Birmingham (1965-78) and National Museum of Wales, Cardiff(1978-86) before becoming a Director of STIPPLE Database Services and Consultant Curator of The Tabley House Collection, University of Manchester. From 1963 he has travelled extensively in Central Europe, in particular Bohemia and Moravia.

Mrs. Caroline Cannon-Brookes studied History of Art at The Courtauld Institute of Art, London University, before taking up a post as Lecturer, University of Leeds (1965-66). Alongside lecturing at the Birmingham College of Art and extensive lecturing for the Extra-Mural Department, University of Birmingham, and the Department of Further Education, University of Oxford, she has led over 60 cultural tours for Martin Randall Travel, specialising in Bohemia, Moravia and Sicily.

Credits

Picture Credits

Ben Uri Collection
Private Collection
Franta Bělský Estate
Studio of Irena Sedlecká
Caroline Uhlman
Benjamin Midgley
Tereza Bušková
Mila Fürstová
Tereza Stehliková

Copyright

28 Freda Salvendy, *Prague*
©Freda Salvendy Estate

30 Käthe, *Village*
©Käthe Strenitz

32 Walter Herz, *Samson*
©Walter Herz Estate

34 Scarlet Nikolska, *Sabbath in Prague*
©Scarlet Nikolska

36 Irena Sedlecká, *Baudelaire in the guise of Faust with the phantom Mephistopheles*
©Studio of Irena Sedlecká

38 Shraga Weil, *Symbols of Passover (The Ram)*
©Shraga Weil Estate

40 Jacob Bornfriend, *Blue Grey Fishes*
©Jacob Bornfriend Estate

42 Yehuda Bacon, *Variations on a Theme*
©Yehuda Bacon

44 Franta Bělský, *Joy-Ride*
©Franta Bělský Estate

46 Franta Bělský, *Pepina*
©Franta Bělský Estate

48 Franta Bělský, *Venusform III*
©Franta Bělský Estate

50 Franta Bělský, *Woman crouching with a mirror*
©Franta Bělský Estate

52 Anita Mandl, *Owl I*
©Anita Mandl

54 Leo Haas, *Ghetto, Terezín-Theresienstadt*
©DACS 2019

56 Leo Haas, *Life, The Market Place, Terezín-Theresienstadt*
©DACS 2019

58 Geza Szobel, *Outside the Prison*
© ADAGP, Paris and DACS, London 2019

60 Irena Sedlecká, *Franz Kafka*
©Studio of Irena Sedlecká

62 Milein Cosman, *John Heartfield*
©Milein Cosman

64 Franta Bělský, *Wenceslas Hollar*
©Franta Bělský Estate

66 Franta Bělský, *Zátopek Military Race Medal*
©Franta Bělský Estate

70 Walter Trier, *Market Woman*
©Walter Trier Estate

72 Frederick Feigl, *The Restaurant*
©Frederick Feigl Estate

74 Irena Sedlecká, *John Gielgud in the role of Hamlet*
©Studio of Irena Sedlecká

76 Irena Sedlecká, *Kenneth Williams*
©Studio of Irena Sedlecká

78 Oskar Kokoschka, *Still-Life Studio Exercise*
©Fondation Oskar Kokoschka/DACS 2019

80 Oskar Kokoschka, *The Donkey*
©Fondation Oskar Kokoschka/ DACS 2019

82 Dorrit Dekk, *'To Tasha'*
©Dorrit Dekk Estate

84 Tereza Bušková, *Erdingtonia*
©Tereza Bušková

88 Mila Fürstová, *Town Tree*
©Mila Fürstová

90 Mila Fürstová, *Nest*
©Mila Fürstová

92 Tereza Stehliková, *Railtracks*
©Tereza Stehliková

All photography
© Justin Piperger
except 84, 88, 90, 92

www.ingramcontent.com/pod-product-compliance
Lightning Source LLC
Chambersburg PA
CBHW050851180526
45159CB00007B/2643